PRAISE FOR *JO*

"With her own style and strong experience with planning, Andrea González helps you bring magic and efficiency in your own paper or digital planner."

—**Virginie Blondeau**, fellow dot journaler

"As someone who regularly uses the technique of dot journaling not only for medical school but for life, I have to say that this book provided me with so many unique ideas and concepts that helped catalyze my productivity! Andrea guides you into organization in the most efficient ways, whether you're a beginner or looking for new tips. The simple, endearing illustrations and content are presented in a way where anyone can understand and apply them! Extremely well done—highly recommended."

—**Sonia**, creator behind @medstu.ies, a journal inspiration platform

"As a teacher, I have always seen how kids struggle with managing their time between school, after school activities, and their social life. This book is the perfect tool to help our kids organize themselves in the active world they live in and succeed on any task they wish to accomplish."

—**Agnes de Dutriz**, teacher

"I enjoyed this book! I wish I would have read it a long time ago. Not only is the journaling system incredible, but the guide to use this and other tools to organize different aspects of my life is absolutely fantastic. Andrea made the journal spreads beautiful and also very functional. Throughout the book she shows a depth of thought and delivers the message in a delightful manner. Just loved it!"

—**Caroll Mercado**, fellow dot journaler

"Uncomplicated, yet thorough!"

—**Ana Isabel Pacas**, fellow dot journaler

"To the point and easy to read. Andrea shares spreads that are easy to put into practice to illustrate the information being shared. Her style is uncomplicated. She emphasizes making the most out of your time, which I think is something a lot of people will relate to. At least, I did. Brilliant!"

—**Mariana**, fellow dot journaler

JOURNAL PLANNING
magic

JOURNAL PLANNING
magic

DOT JOURNALING FOR CALM,
 CREATIVITY, AND
CONQUERING YOUR GOALS

ANDREA GONZÁLEZ, CREATOR OF
PLAN FOR PRODUCTIVITY

CORAL GABLES

Cover Design: Elina Diaz and Andrea González
Cover Photo/illustration: Andrea González
Layout & Design: Elina Diaz

For permission requests, please contact the publisher at:
Mango Publishing Group
2850 S Douglas Road, 2nd Floor
Coral Gables, FL 33134 USA
info@mango.bz

For special orders, quantity sales, course adoptions and corporate sales, please email the publisher at sales@mango.bz. For trade and wholesale sales, please contact Ingram Publisher Services at customer.service@ingramcontent.com or +1.800.509.4887.

Journal Planning Magic: Dot Journaling for Calm, Creativity, and Conquering Your Goals

Library of Congress Cataloging-in-Publication number: 2020940930
ISBN: (print) 978-1-64250-350-0, (ebook) 978-1-64250-351-7
BISAC category code: GAM021000—GAMES & ACTIVITIES / Guided Journals

Printed in the United States of America

Para Papi:

Above all, you taught me what it means to be happy.
I don't need any plans for that.

"What we achieve inwardly will change outer reality."

—Plutarch

Table of Contents

PART I

Your Recipe for Planning Success

INTRODUCTION

Why We Plan

If I'm being completely honest, I plan because I was taught to. My amazing mom is a planner at heart. I grew up seeing meal plans magnetized to the fridge, vacations booked two years in advance, and Excel sheets that would account for every penny spent in the house. I learned at a very early age the value of being prepared. My mom taught me that planning wasn't an activity as much as it was a lifestyle and a mindset. Planning carries you through life with a bit less of uncertainty and a bit more of achieving your goals. Your plans, however big or small, are the reason you are where you are today.

I was lucky. It was because of her that I plan. But, why do I keep doing it? Why is planning still so valuable in my life? Why do I want to teach you the magic of planning?

It was when I learned *how* to plan that I started seeing big changes in my life. I started dot journaling when a friend suggested that, since I was pretty much obsessed with planning already, I might really enjoy customizing my calendars and satisfying my Obsessive-Compulsive personality. I immediately fell in love with it. Little did I know, I was starting a journey of obsessing over planning strategies and researching every possible detail about how to become a better version of myself. It's a journey that's just beginning, by the way.

It was when I learned to plan that I started to grow in multiple areas of my life, not just my "career." I started to discover who I want to be. I started to set goals, build habits, and shape the person I am. More importantly, I started achieving things that I only ever dreamed of doing. When people ask me how I did this, I scanned my memory for the hardships and struggles, playing in my mind the long, tedious movie of my self-improvement journey, and—to my surprise—couldn't find anything. But one day, as I was looking for a random spread in one of my old journals, I found the answer to that question. The evidence was right in front of me: monthly goals, habit trackers, weekly plans, daily prioritization...a color-coded story of how I got to where I am today.

Goals sometimes seem so unattainable. Planning is the magic wand with which you bring them back to earth. A *swish* here, a *flick* there, and the path to achieving a daunting dream appears right in front of you, in a 5" by 8" dotted journal. Let me teach you how to swish and flick. Let me show you that it's not as overwhelming as you think. Let me help you reach those goals.

The motivational speaker and productivity expert Simon Sinek explained in an interview the difference between planning in the military and business. He said, "Planning is something that happens—in business—either once a year or when something goes wrong. In the military, they're constantly, constantly, constantly planning. [In business,] planning is an event, not a process." Planning is a process because growth is a process. If you want to be in control of who you are, what you do, and how you grow, you need to plan for it. Constantly. This, unfortunately, is why I think so many people shy away from planning. It seems tedious, overwhelming, even. I get it. But it doesn't have to be. It can be simple, and you can make it your own. If you learn the tools in this book and make planning a process—a routine part of your life—then you will have the means to always keep growing.

"Now I think it's one of the most useless questions an adult can ask a child—What do you want to be when you grow up? As if growing up is finite. As if at some point you become something and that's the end."

—Michelle Obama, *Becoming*

Are you ready to become a planner? Let go of any assumptions you've made and any biases you may have. I'll show you that planning doesn't have to be complicated. I'll walk you through every step of the way. Let's start fresh. To get started, I recommend buying a blank journal. When you're ready, turn to the first page of your empty notebook. Let's start designing your life.

HOW TO GET THE MOST OUT OF THIS BOOK

If possible, start journaling now. If there's anything that resonates with you, I suggest you start implementing it in the moment. Use the templates (or do it in your own journal), highlight the book, and get involved. Apply what you learn as you read the book. By the end, you'll be an expert at planning.

Find what works for you. Don't feel obligated to do everything mentioned in this book. Instead, find what can complement your current way of doing things. Do the things that will serve you best. Focus on the principles more than the tools and come up with the perfect planning system for you. Get creative!

Reach out. We're all in this journey together, and each one of us brings something special to the table. Share what you create with the hashtag **#planningmagic**. Ask questions, leave comments, give ideas, help others, and share your insight with the rest of us. I can't wait to be inspired by you.

CHAPTER 1

The Somewhat Misunderstood Bullet Journal Method

If you bought this book, you've most likely heard of The Bullet Journal Method. If you haven't, well...your life's about to change. In the shortest possible summary, the BuJo (the internet's abbreviation for Bullet Journal) method is an analog system created by Ryder Carroll that allows you to keep all of your thoughts in one place: a notebook. Usually a dotted one, hence the common term "dot journal."

A BuJo is basically a set of tools that allows you to organize your ideas, tasks, memories, and pretty much anything else that you can think of. A single notebook becomes a combination of your calendar, your planner, your task list, your often-misplaced Post-it notes, your journal, your habit tracker, your place for midnight ideas on a napkin, your random notes, your responsibilities...essentially, your life. My journal is basically my second brain, which in turn means my actual brain has a lot less work to do.

Unfortunately, if you google "Bullet Journal," the first thing you'll see is wildly time consuming spreads (a spread is just any template you've created on your journal), detailed calendars, fancy lettering that seemingly only an artist could ever create, and a fairly large pile of supplies neatly placed next to the notebook... That is not what Bullet Journaling is about! Don't get me wrong, the creative aspect is one of my favorite parts of BuJo, but there is so much more (or perhaps *less*) to this method. After years of experience, I'm convinced that Bullet Journaling is almost a mindset. It's a decision to live your life intentionally. To, as Carroll says, "Track the Past, Order the Present, Design the Future." You need no artistic skill to succeed at Bullet Journaling. The desire to take control of your life will suffice. If you want to decorate, however, the journal can most certainly be your canvas, and planning your life can be the creative ritual you've been missing.

THE BUJO FRAMEWORK

In this section, I'm going to briefly explain The Bullet Journal Method, summing up Carroll's own words. If you're a BuJo pro, you can go ahead and skip this, although I found it very refreshing to go back to the basics of Bullet Journaling as I read through this section of his book. Once you've got the gist of what the system is like (and hopefully you've put it into practice for a few days) we can get into the nitty gritty details of planning and making this method your own.

What follows might seem like a set of instructions and a relatively boring and rigid set of terms and definitions, but don't worry, there is light at the end of the tunnel. The BuJo method is the opposite of rigid. Unfortunately, we have to explain/ understand the system before we can get into the fun stuff. A quick tip that will make this slightly more enjoyable: open your journal and get started with me!

COLLECTIONS

Your journal will be composed of Collections. In summary, a Collection is a page with a title made specifically for logging content related to that title. Carroll describes them as "the modular building blocks of BuJo, used to store related content." The core Collections of the system are the Index, the Future Log, the Monthly Log, and the Daily Log. Once you start to use your journal on a regular basis, you'll notice that you'll be inclined to create Collections for anything you might need. It can be a themed list, a tracker, or the canvas for an idea you are trying to develop. You can create one for anything you want to keep track of.

INDEX

Because your journal will be the home to almost anything that goes through your mind, the first collection in your notebook will be the Index. There's not much science to this; it's page numbers with their corresponding page titles. I'm pretty sure you've seen one of these before. There's one at the beginning of this book!

FUTURE LOG

This is where your future commitments live. The basic structure is a set of pages that contain the upcoming months with some space to jot down notes in. Any task, event, or project that falls outside of the current month can be logged into your future log.

For example, under June, you might write: "15th—Road trip for Angel's birthday."

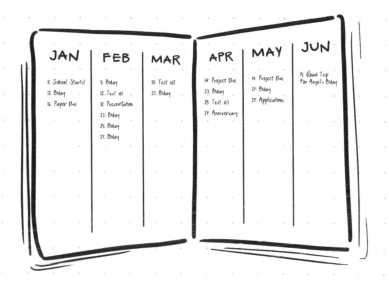

Example of a Future Log

MONTHLY LOG

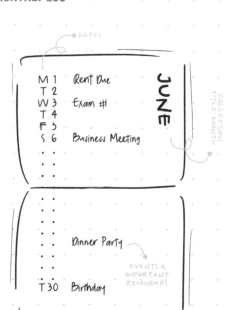

An overview of the current month. This is where you can jot down the tasks and events you've scheduled for that month. All you need is a list from one to thirty (or however many day are in that month) and some space to write your commitments next to the date.

DAILY LOG

According to Carroll, the Daily Log "serves as your catchall for Rapid Logging your thoughts throughout each day." This is basically the space where you capture your thoughts, tasks, events, and notes for the day. The title of this collection is simply the day's date. Under it, you would add, for example, your morning workout, your 2:00 p.m. meeting, after-work plans, and house chores to do today.

KEY INGREDIENTS

Here are a few more terms you might want to get familiar with. If you choose to use the BuJo method, these play a huge role in how you use your journal on a regular basis. These three concepts are something I've noticed most seasoned Bullet Journalers out there tend to forget about. Understanding the purpose behind each of these practices will turn your journal from an organizational tool to a life design notebook.

RAPID LOGGING

This is the essence of Bullet Journaling. According to Ryder Carroll, rapid logging involves "using short-form notation paired with symbols to quickly capture, categorize, and prioritize your thoughts into Notes, Events, and Tasks." The whole point of this organization system is so that you can literally have a thought and log it *rapidly* onto the next blank space in your journal. No friction, no censorship. Just log.

REFLECTION

This is the practice of reviewing and revising your journal without any other distractions. There are two ideal times for reflection: morning and evening. The idea is just to sit down with pen and paper to think about your life for a few minutes, and usually, migrate your notes.

MIGRATION

This is the monthly process of filtering out meaningless content from your notebook. In my opinion, migration happens whenever you look back through your journal and make a decision about what you are going to transfer to your next spread. You can migrate today's tasks into tomorrow's Daily Log, you can migrate into the following month, you can even migrate into your next journal.

This process is where the magic happens. This slight pause in your day, reflecting upon every task or note that you want to transfer, is what will allow you to live an intentional life.

THE BULLETS

I mean, it is called *Bullet* Journaling for a reason. This symbol system will allow you to log rapidly. Instead of having to explain what a thought is with words, you'll add a symbol before it to identify it as a task, event, or note.

- Task
- O Event
- — Note

So, at a glance, you can see everything you might have logged that day. This will not only save you time, but it will encourage you to log pretty much anything that goes through your head.

Now you don't have to think about where a thought goes—they all go in your Bullet Journal—you just have to identify if it is a task, event, or note. This also makes looking back at your journal easy and enjoyable. You'll be able to spot pretty quickly whatever you're looking for.

Along with the basic bullets for tasks, events, and notes, there are signifiers that will help you identify the things that are important or urgent.

★   Important

!   Urgent

Carroll created a key for the system, but you can create your own, of course! Play around; find what comes naturally to you. Find something that is easy to understand at a glance and that makes you happy to look at. (Or am I the only person that finds neatly stacked symbols satisfying? The symbols that you use don't matter as long as you have something to distinguish all the categories of your life (tasks, events, notes). For example, as a student, I created an extra bullet to represent exams.

☐   Exams

I wanted it to be very clear when I had an exam coming up and did not want it to get mixed up with classes or other appointments. I've seen people create bullets to separate work-related appointments from personal ones. Maybe you want a specific symbol to represent a memory for that day, or a symbol to represent an idea, so you know to follow up on it when you have more time. I have a bunch of different signifiers and bullets for all the things I want to be able to identify at a glance.

This is my current key:

my key

· TASK	● COMPLETED	* IMPORTANT
○ EVENT	✓ STARTED	! URGENT
− NOTE	› MIGRATED	~ MAYBE
+ MORE	‹ SCHEDULED	◔ DUE
	× CANCELLED	◈ IDEA

I place emphasis on the word *current*. Your key will change; it will evolve to suit your present needs, which inevitably will change as well. For example, I no longer have a symbol for exams, since I don't have nearly as many as I did for the past five years. Who knows, maybe by the time this book is published my key will have changed again. Don't worry, I'm sure I'm going to share it on my social media page, Plan for Productivity, in case you're interested. Now, it's your turn, go to the first page of your journal and create your own key.

THE SUM OF THE PARTS

Each of these parts of the system is important, crucial, even, to make sure that your life's plans live within your journal. The key is essential for rapid logging, the migration is essential to keep track of everything you are welcoming into your life, and so on. They are all connected.

So, how does it look in action?

Well, let's start today. Open up your journal and title your collection Monday, January 4th, or whatever day you are actually reading this. What is one thing that you want to accomplish today? Write that task down. Where do you have to be today? Write that event down. Throughout the day, as you come up with more things to get done, just write them down with your task bullet in front of them. If a thought comes to mind, write it down...yes, there, under your tasks... If you have an idea, write it down! Do you see where I'm going with this?

Let's say today you're told you have a project due on March 18th—where does that piece of information go? In your Future Log, under March! Or, if you're short on time, you can write it down right there in today's log, and at the end of the day, you can transfer that into your Future Log. The idea is to use your Daily Log as a notepad for all of today's thoughts, regardless of whether those come in the form of tasks, events, ideas, notes, emotions, information, or whatever it is you're thinking.

Now let's fast forward to night time, when you've left half of those tasks undone and all your notes in almost impossible-to-comprehend scribbles. Now it's time to "Reflect" on your day. This is when you take a look at the items in your Daily Log and decide what you're going to do with them—where do they belong? This is where these symbols come in.

>   <   ×

For example, let's take my Daily Log for January 13. There are a few tasks left "unchecked" or with an "open" task bullet. For each of these, I'm going to decide if I want to get this done tomorrow, if it should be scheduled for the distant future, or if it should no longer be a part of my life. I'll use Carroll's system. Let's see how that works:

>   "Create content calendar." This, for example, is something I believe to be important because it will allow me to create better content for my audience and help me get it all done in advance, so I can stay consistent. Even though I did not

get to it today, I believe this is something I most definitely want to get done, therefore I will *migrate* it onto tomorrow's log. To signify this, I turned the dot bullet into a forward arrow, meaning I moved it forward into tomorrow.

< "Diana's Birthday on February 5" is an event that is coming up in the future, therefore I will transfer this into my Future Log. To illustrate this, I turned the dot bullet into a backward arrow meaning I have *scheduled* it in my Future Log (back in the first pages of my journal). This will help keep your Future Log up to date with any events you might have coming up.

× "Define group project objectives." This task, for example, I realized was not something I should be doing. I could delegate this to my classmate who has more experience doing this, and I can focus on another part of the project, where I'll be more useful. I placed an X over the bullet to signify that this is a *cancelled* task, and I no longer need or want this to be a part of my to-do list.

Next, I wrote paragraphs explaining *why* I migrated, scheduled, or cancelled tasks. This proccess of deciding what to do with a given task takes only a few seconds and the more you do it, the more natural it'll feel. This brief pause, however, is life-changing.

Because you have to rewrite any unfinished tasks in your next day's log, you are forced to look at a task and make a decision. Are you going to include it in tomorrow's list, or are you going to cross it out of your life? Is it worth your time? Is it even worth the thirty seconds it might take you to rewrite it? See, most apps will do this automatically, with the intention of shaving a few seconds off your day, but those seconds matter. These seconds embrace the practice of mindfulness and intentionality. When you are rewriting a task onto the next day, you are making the conscious decision of including it in tomorrow's intentions. You are saying yes to that task and to spending your time completing it. The same happens when you cancel a task. Sometimes, the things we say no to are more important than the things we say yes to. When you choose to X out an item, you are prioritizing something else—you are acknowledging that this item is no longer important to you, and therefore you want it out of your journal, out of your mind. These few seconds of your day provide you with the space to become intentional about how you are going to live tomorrow.

Most scheduling software will migrate tasks for you, but it will eliminate the choices and automatically transfer all your open tasks to the next day's intention list. The days go by, and your to-do list keeps getting bigger and bigger, full of meaningless five-minute tasks that carry no weight on your goals, that will drive you nowhere in particular, and make you feel like you've accomplished nothing in the past month. Yeah, we've all been there.

By rewriting a task over and over again, you'll become aware that you might be postponing something. Why? Why haven't I done that in the past ten days? Should I even be doing it? Does it need to get done? Is this pure procrastination? Am I going to cross it out or finally get it done? This awareness of your habits and tendencies is powerful. It's going to change your life. And yes, eventually, it will come naturally. So, keep reading.

Anyway, I digress—a quick recap: jot down whatever comes to mind, and at the end of the day, take a few minutes to reflect and redirect your tasks into their corresponding collections.

Now that you've learned the fundamentals of this system, you're ready for the next step, making this practice your own. Don't forget to keep using your journal as you go along so you can tailor this system to what comes instinctively to you.

CHAPTER 2

One Day at a Time

You live your life one day at a time. Literally. There is no way around that, there is no way to skip a few hours. All you can do is live that day, breathe for twenty-four hours, and repeat when the next day starts. So if you're gonna be breathing anyway, why not make it the best possible day...every single day? It's that simple...all you have to do is basically make it through the 1,440 minutes of the day, for the 365 days of the year, for the eighty-ish years of your life. Isn't math amazing? If only reality added up just as nicely...

Seriously though, the "secret" to living your best life—from what I've learned so far—is to create it on a regular basis. It's not about being perfect, or overworking yourself, or assigning a task for every time slot in your calendar. It's not about learning every possible little detail there is to learn about organization, planning, prioritization, time management and whatever new skill the world just came up with. It's about knowing yourself so that you can *plan* the ideal day that will suit your needs and that will take you, at a realistic pace, towards the life you aim to build. You achieve your dreams by spending time on them on a daily basis.

There is no one-size-fits-all recipe to a "productive" day. There are so many variables that will influence how you organize it, from the kind of job you have, what your schedule is like, how much of your schedule you can control, how much sleep you got the day before to whether you are an early bird or a night owl or even the time you like to have breakfast. So, as you can guess from this extensive intro, I will not give you the recipe for a perfect day. Instead, I will give you the tools I believe are essential to creating a daily routine that fits your lifestyle. And, of course, teach you along the way about how your journal can help with that.

THE DAILY LOG

This is the page in your notebook that has today's date as a title. This is where you'll capture your thoughts for today, your tasks, events, notes, ideas, any piece of information you might get—and anything that is worth writing down—can be logged here, for the day.

This collection serves two purposes, in my opinion.

1. To plan out and organize the day ahead.

2. To safely capture your thoughts throughout the day.

So, these two functions are what we'll attempt to master in this chapter. If you've come up with a third one, don't hesitate to share! I'm all for new ideas here.

When I started Bullet Journaling, I would set up spaces to for multiple Daily Logs in one page, more or less like what a planner looks like:

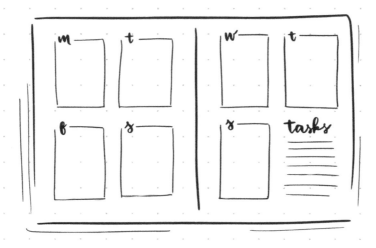

Or what the internet calls a Weekly Log. I'll discuss this more later on, but for now I just wanted to remind you that the beauty and functionality of the Daily Log relies on not limiting the space to capture your thoughts. One day you might fill half a page, another day you might fill three pages worth of today's Rapid Logging. This is what will allow you to capture every thought without judgement and without hesitation. If you have to pause and think if something important enough to write in the ten lines' worth of space you have left for today's log, then you will be reluctant to capture every thought. There should be no friction whatsoever when it comes to capturing a thought. It should be as easy as possible to write it down, which is why you might want to use Rapid Logging to capture it in today's Daily Log and sort it out later.

INGREDIENTS FOR PRODUCTIVITY POTION

How can you become *truly* productive? To answer that, we'll start with the first purpose the Daily Log serves: organizing your day. Even the most disorganized, messy, unstructured rebels organize their day. When I talk about structuring your day, however, I don't only mean adding events to the calendar and setting alarms to avoid that most embarrassing walk of shame into a meeting when late. I mean finding the time and organizing your time so you'll be able to do the things that matter *to* you, in the most efficient way *for* you. In order to have a productive day, you have to really understand *why* you are choosing to do something. If you are working on something you truly believe in, no one can tell you your day was "unproductive," not even yourself.

Before we get into the details of calendars and tables and bullets, let's build a good foundation as to why you are doing things a certain way. Here are a few concepts that I think will help you get some clarity in your day. I call these The Principles of Productivity. These mindset shifts are what allowed me to exponentially increase my "productivity." They are rules that I can fall back on when I'm feeling lost and unfocused. These virtues have become the building blocks over which I structure my day in order to take the most advantage of my time on this earth. And, I know they can do the same for you. Most of the time, it's not the lack of plans that leave us feeling like there are not enough hours in the day; it's the lack of intention and ingenuity in our plans. Let's fix that.

HONOR YOUR COMMITMENTS

You would think that when you wake up in the morning, your to-do list is an empty piece of paper; however, that's not really the case... Normally, by the time you get to planning the day, you already have things you are supposed to accomplish. You might have places you have to be, projects that are due, or things that just have get done. The point is, even though you might not be aware of them, you already have things planned. You already made previous commitments that you must show up for. So, hopefully you can make yourself aware of what these things are *before* you start adding tasks to today's Daily Log.

This means that when it comes to planning your day, the first thing you have to account for and add to your Daily Log are your previous commitments. What is already on your schedule for today, and at what time are those appointments happening? This will leave you with a pretty good idea of how many hours you have left to work on other tasks.

> **Magic Trick:** I try to make myself aware of what these commitments are the night before, so I'm not too lost in the morning.

Now, there are many ways to do this in your journal. You can use Carroll's method and simply write them down with the event bullet in front of them without any order in particular. You can also create a timeline for the day and block out the times when those appointments are scheduled. You can write the time slots right next to the event, so you don't miss them. You can do what I do: I add them to my journal with the event bullet *and* chuck them into my digital calendar, so I get reminders and can visually see them on a timeline. Or you can create a little system of your own. It doesn't matter as long as you are aware that those specific hours of the day have already been assigned to an event. When you open up your journal to plan your day, it should be easy to picture what portions of your day are free or busy.

SEPTEMBER 7

- ○ birthday dinner @ 7pm
- ○ meeting @ 2pm

- • task #1
- • task #2
- • task #3

SEPTEMBER 7

- [2PM] meeting
- [7PM] birthday dinner

- • task #1
- • task #2
- • task #3

SEPTEMBER 7

1
2 · meeting
3 ·
4
5
6
7 · birthday dinner
8

This step is important because it will define the number of tasks you might want to add to your Daily Log. Let's say, today, you have scheduled a 7:00 a.m. gym class, then your 9-to-5 job, and then you have a one-hour doctor's appointment at 6:00 p.m. Well, today is pretty packed and it looks like you don't have much to accomplish the fifteen things you want to get to sometime soon. Most people will write the fifteen things in today's to-do list anyway. Would you? Are you sure? No! Don't write the fifteen things in today's list. All that's going to do is waste your time and leave you feeling unsuccessful at the end of the day. Instead, let's prioritize and *realistically* add the tasks to your Daily Log that you might actually accomplish today with the little time you have left. Don't worry, we'll talk more about how to do this in the next few pages.

More importantly, however, there is power, authority and value in a person that does what they said they were going to do. A lot of people can blabber on about their plans, but can they actually follow through? Every single time you pass on doing something you have previously committed to do, you are rewiring your brain to believe that you can't actually stick to your plans and get stuff done. Even if it's "only" a commitment with yourself that you've missed. Even if no one else knows, you are crushing your self-confidence. If you are constantly rescheduling your plans, then you'll never achieve anything by its due date. So, knowing what it is you planned for your day in advance so you can honor those commitments and follow through is a huge advantage over the sixty-something percent of the world who wake up with no road to follow towards their goals. Did you do what you said you were going to do? Did you follow through?

EMBRACE YOUR CHRONOTYPE

In his book *When: The Scientific Secrets of Perfect Timing*, Daniel Pink writes about three chronotypes. Two of these are widely known: Larks and Owls. Larks are the people who do their best, most focused work in the morning. They don't have a problem waking up while it's still dark outside and usually feel energized in the mornings. Owls are the complete opposite. These are the people who do their best work at night. The moon is their sun, and they are not afraid of the dark at all. The third chronotype, however, was something I had never heard of. He calls these people the Third Birds. These are the people who wake up "at a normal time," not too early, yet still get their peaks of energy mid-morning. They also do their best work during the day. This is actually where the majority of the people fit in.

In the book, Pink mentions a simple test to get a better idea of what your chronotype is: At what time do you normally wake up during the weekends? If you naturally wake up at dawn, you're probably a Lark. If you wake up around nine, you're probably a Third Bird, and if you sleep in past noon, you're most likely an Owl.

So, the idea is that based on what you're chronotype is there may be a better time of the day for you to do certain tasks. When you are trying to tackle an analytical task, you need deep focus, fresh eyes, and a lot of brain power. On the contrary, if you are trying to tackle a more creative task, while still quite energy-consuming, you need your inhibitions a bit lowered, less structure, and a more free flowing train of thought. This is why Pink suggests that Larks and Third Birds should try to tackle their analytical work in the mornings and their creative tasks in the afternoon, and Owls should try to tackle their analytical tasks at night and their creative work in the mornings.

How many times have you been told that you should do your most important task first? Yep, me too. Sometimes, we try so hard to work on the thing we "have to get done first" just because that is what we've always been told, when in reality, your brain might not be at its prime, in the moment, to be focusing on that task. You spend hours and hours trying to accomplish that one task without really making any progress, and before you know it, you've wasted half your morning. This theory provides you with an alternative way to organize your tasks: according to the time when your mind is better prepared to complete *that specific task*. By adhering to this organization trick, it may even take less effort to accomplish that task. There's so much freedom in that.

Back in the industrial age, productivity used to be measured as a function of time. Most people would work jobs that did not require too much attention, focus, or creative energy; therefore, the more time you would put into the work, the more you would produce. In our modern world, however, most of us are doing creative and analytical work that requires a lot of brain power. This is why in the book, *The Productivity Project*, Chris Bailey proposes that productivity is the product of managing your time, attention, and energy equally. Knowing how to manage your time could very well be useless if you don't have enough energy to dedicate your undivided attention to a specific task you meant to get done from 9:00 to 10:00 a.m. This is where embracing your chronotype can make a world of a difference in your productivity. Knowing at what times you work best can provide you with the energy that you're missing to get things done to the best of your abilities. The next time you are having trouble moving forward with a task, ask yourself, "Is it that I didn't give myself enough time to complete it, or that within that work window, I am unable to really focus and be as effective as I should to get this done?"

Of course, this is just a guideline. Some of us don't have the flexibility to rearrange our days however we please because we have a schedule to stick to or a job to punch in at. Sometimes that makes it impossible for you to even have your "prime work hours" free to dedicate to your priorities. But, whenever you can, try embrace your chronotype and organize your schedule in a way that work for you.

This theory is not a strict don't-color-outside-the-lines recipe, this is a guide, a path for you to follow. More than obliging by these guidelines, the lesson here is to know yourself. Know *when* you do your best work so you can shield your energy from mindless, insignificant tasks and spend it on the things that require your undivided attention and energy. Stop shooting yourself in the foot; just take advantage of your internal clock as much as possible.

Once you've understood when you'll be doing your best work, it's time to decide *what* it is you'll be doing at that time. Enter: Priorities.

LET GO OF THE BUSY IDENTITY

Of the examples below, which person's journal do you "admire" the most? Quick, don't think, just answer! Which person do you think was more productive that day?

SEPTEMBER 25

☑ Answer email

- · cook lunch
- ● call mom
- ● clean bathroom
- ● tidy desk drawers
- · catch up on tv show
- · read 1 article
- ● wash dishes
- · 1 load of laundry
- ●. dinner reservations
- ● order stock items
- ●. upload insta story
- · film 1 youtube video

SEPTEMBER 25

☑ Plan next month's content

- ● 1 hr of personal finance course
- ● meal prep for the week
- ● 2 hrs side business work

The fast pace of the modern world has embedded in our brain that "busy" equals productive, which equals successful. How many of us answer the question, "how are you doing," with "great, but busy?" I'm definitely guilty of this. Somewhere along the way we started to believe that the more things we have to do, the more things we check off our to-do list, the more "successful" we are, at least in other people's eyes. Lexie Harvey mentions in her TED Talk regarding this issue, "Business has become the essence of success and failure is [now] equated with how much free time someone has." People wear the busy identity with pride, it makes us feel important. I mean, it makes sense... the more we have to do must mean the more significant our job is.

Harvey goes on to say that people "have taken it upon themselves to cram their schedules in order to feel more important." We might even be doing this subconsciously, without even realizing that we could eliminate probably half of the things on our to-do lists and nothing would change. We create long lists to reinforce the belief that we are in fact very busy and don't have time for any of those big, maybe even more important things we'd like to do (much like the first image above), but when you look at it closely, how many of these things matter? How many of these things will have a significant impact on your future? In my opinion, maybe the less "busy" person had a more significant day, given that the three things they did that day were "big" tasks that have great significance in their future.

When journaling, we may be tempted to fill our page with tasks so that it looks like we had a productive, busy day; the objective, though, is to do the opposite. We want to eliminate as many tasks as we possibly can, either by delegating them, batching them, or flat out crossing them out. And, we want to add to our task lists the things that might actually move the needle for us in some way.

By being intentional, focusing on the things that matter, and looking not only at today's task list, but at your notes, your journal entries, your goals, your thoughts, and your entire journal, you can start to see what things actually have an impact in your life, and, therefore, the ones you should prioritize. Through dot journaling, you can disconnect your day's value from the number of things you crossed off your list, and you can disconnect that part of your self-worth that is tied to how busy you are. Life is about way more than checking boxes and accomplishing tasks. Instead of focusing our journaling practice on the menial tasks we "have" to do, let's focus it on discovering who we want to be, what makes us happy, and how we want to *live* our lives.

Carlin Daharsh reminds us in her TED Talk "Too Busy for Productivity" that "the most successful people are known for *one* great achievement, not a million great achievements." While this seems unbelievably obvious, it was something I had completely forgotten about. I've always been interested in pretty much everything. I like trying new things, diving into a million projects at a time, and trying to include a little bit of everything in my day. While I am a fairly logical person, and studying was never really an issue for me (until I landed in medical school), I am also a fairly creative person. This, I see now, is really my natural state: it engages my mind, keeps me interested and makes me forget that I'm hungry. Which, you know, is a pretty significant sign that you're enjoying what you are doing...or is that just me? Anyway, my theory was that I could always have *everything.* That I could be great at everything, that time was a made-up concept and I could bend, fold, and twist it to whatever shape or form I needed. I'd be able to do all those things I put on my plate. Poor seventeen-year-old me.

Med School: "You think you have time for everything? Well, here's everything you have to read, all the places you have to be, all the things you have to know, and a pitcher of guilt for whenever you feel like relaxing. Go." Fun times... Anyway, I quickly learned that time is, of course, limited and extremely valuable and that learning to prioritize should be my number one priority. I learned that what I spend my time and energy on determines who I am. Given my unfocused nature, my mom would always tell me, *"El que mucho abarca poco aprieta."* I have no clue how to translate this into English, but it means something along the lines of, "If you try to do too many things at the same time, you won't be able to master any of them." Yes Mom, you were right. But it wasn't until I discovered the Bullet Journal that I could see *what* to focus on. Through writing everything down, I was able to understand what "tasks" matter, what things actually play a significant role in my daily life, and what I can eliminate to focus on the one thing (or three things, I mean, come on—it used to be ten) that I might become "great" at.

Unfortunately, in the modern world of sharing a very much edited version of your life every minute of the day, we lack awareness about what really matters. Our society has pushed us to believe that *everything* matters, from what car you own to what color of mug you drink your morning coffee in. Every. Little. Detail. Worse, it has made us believe that we have to be perfect at everything and that we have to be the best possible version in all areas of your life. Can anyone really work a 9-to-5 job, take care of four children, keep the house obsessively clean, feed their family three times a day in a perfectly arranged dinner table, oh, without repeating any meals, work on a side business, be the perfect wife, contribute to their community, go to church every Sunday, have a perfectly decorated house, exercise every day, sleep eight hours a day, drive their kids to myriad after school activities, hang out with friends, be incredibly patient and nice to every single mean person they meet, etc.?

I could go on and on with the list of expectations for every possible area of your life. It's endless. Something's gotta give, and it can't be your health, it can't be your family, and it can't be your source of income, so it has to be this idea of living a picture-perfect life. Instead, choose intention, choose purpose, and choose to follow your why. Whatever doesn't align with any of your goals, let it go. Focus on what matters to you.

So how do we fight this busy identity? Prioritizing.

PRIORITIZATION PARTY: YOU'RE INVITED!

What's the ultimate guide to prioritization? There isn't one.

Okay, all joking aside. There isn't really one way to prioritize because everyone's priorities are different, and they can vary on daily basis. Some people need to base them off of urgency, others off of what has the most impact. What works for me may not work for you. There are a few systems that might help you understand what your priorities are, and I'll explain three in this chapter. You can use them when facing a massive, overwhelming list of things to get done. Just like anything that takes practice, the more you do it, the easier it will become, to the point that you might not need a system to prioritize your tasks. Eventually, it'll just be second nature.

THE EISENHOWER MATRIX

This is probably the most famous prioritization technique, popularized by Stephen R. Covey in his book *The 7 Habits of Highly Effective People.* The idea is that for each task, you must decide if it's important or not and if it's urgent or not. Once you've assigned each task to a designated space in the matrix, you want to do the corresponding action for each cell. I've redrawn a version of the matrix here for you and added some notes of my own to give you some guidance.

THE EISENHOWER MATRIX

	IMPORTANT	NOT IMPORTANT
URGENT	**DO** Prioritize these tasks.	**DELEGATE** These tasks don't require your specific skills, delegate them. If you can't, find ways to be better prepared in the future.
NOT URGENT	**SCHEDULE** Plan and decide when the best time to work on these tasks is and add it to your calendar!	**ELIMINATE** Don't do them at all. If necessary, designate the best time to get them done.

It's pretty simple and easy to refer back to when you don't know what to do with a specific task, or maybe you don't know how to start tackling your to-do list. There are two ways in which I use this. First, I use it when I get so anxious just from looking at my to-do list that I procrastinate until I actually have something to be anxious about... For these extensive lists, I'll categorize each of the items into the matrix and take it from there. Second, I use the matrix when I don't know how much of a priority an item in my list is. For each of these puzzling tasks, I'll ask myself "Is it important? Is it urgent?" And I usually get a better idea of when that task should get done. As you can see, I *do not* do this every day for every to-do list I make; that would be incredibly cumbersome. But if you have no clue how to prioritize your action list, this is a simple place to start. Let me give you an example:

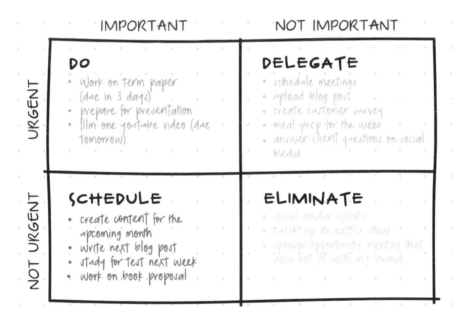

ADD A SPRINKLE OF MAGIC

One random, let's say Tuesday, night, I was feeling a bit unfocused and lacking any motivation to study. Naturally, I turned to YouTube for a quick dose of endorphins and encouragement to fix my issue. As I eagerly scrolled through YouTube—not procrastinating, of course—I stumbled upon a TED Talk titled "How to Multiply Your Time" by the author of the book *Procrastinate on Purpose*, Rory Vaden. Of course, from the title alone, I was hooked. *Should I take a break from not studying by clicking on a twenty-minute video that might "help me somehow," yet might also leave me simply wanting to spiral down for another hour on this fascinatingly addictive social media platform? Why not*? Ladies and gentlemen: The YouTube Trap. Anyway, I clicked on the video. Well...those twenty minutes I "wasted" changed my life.

Vaden starts his talk by explaining how the world of productivity has evolved. In the '50s, it was all about efficiency. If we could do things faster and more efficiently, we could get more done. He calls this one-dimensional thinking. Around the '80s, it developed into two-dimensional thinking, based on importance and urgency. Sound familiar? Yes, he is talking about the Eisenhower Matrix. According to Vanden's theory, though, the problem with this approach to productivity is that is does not create more time, it only reorganizes the things you have to do. It borrows time from one activity to spend on another. Which, by the way, is still an essential skill.

So, to solve this dilemma, we employ three-dimensional thinking. This is the magical element that modernized the Eisenhower Matrix. Here, we ask not only how important or urgent something is, but also how significant. Rory explains it best:

> *"If importance is how much something matters and urgency is how soon it matters, significance is how long it's going to matter."*

Read that again. What can you do today that will make tomorrow better? Essentially, how would you like to *invest* your time? In other words, he says, "You multiply your time by giving yourself the emotional permission to invest time into things today that will create more time and more results for tomorrow."

We're so eager to jump into the hamster wheel of ticking off to-do's and getting things done and busying ourselves. We so easily fall into this urgency trap of only following through at the last possible minute. We are running through life trying to catch up to the rapid rhythm, yet we're always a step behind.

Let me paint you a gorgeous picture. Second semester of medical school, about five years ago, young, restless little me was excited to finally jump into the more "advanced" medical courses. That semester was composed of four classes: Anatomy, Histology, Chemistry, and Physics. After organizing the schedule, we ended up with about one exam per week with the occasional back-to-back or two-days-apart exams. So, the first exam week of that semester, all of us would pour out our hearts, pass on sleep, read hundreds of pages worth of content, and fry our brains studying for the Anatomy test only to have a short bad night's rest and start all over again the next day for the upcoming Chemistry test, then again for the Histology test, then cram months of content into forty-eight hours for the Physics test and then repeat the cycle over and over and over again until the end of final exams. I was eating whatever junk I could find. I was furnished with pimples and radiated anxiety. I get chills just thinking about it... We were crawling, trying to catch up, never quite on top of things, never quite prepared, never slowing down. Most of my friends didn't even know what next week's test was because they were so enclosed by the urgency of this week's exam.

By the time the next ruthless semester of my career came along, I knew better. As early as possible, I created a calendar (I hadn't discovered the Bullet Journal yet) with all the upcoming exams. I logged the lectures we received and started reviewing them one at a time, investing no more than one or two hours a day. I arranged my schedule so that by the time an exam week came up, I would have already studied most of the topics for that test. The day before the exam, my friends would ask me, "How can you possibly be studying for another subject if the test is tomorrow!?" The answer was simple. This week's test no longer felt urgent to me. If I started studying for the next subject, by the time that test came along, I wouldn't have to cram, either. And that turned out to be true—I didn't study a single weekend that semester. Which, believe me, is a huge statement in medical school. Everyone says that semester was dreadful, but it felt like a breeze to me. I was on top of things because I learned firsthand that all the things you do today shape tomorrow. I gave myself the permission to let go of that feeling of urgency so that I could focus on the things that would keep me afloat in the future. This is an obvious concept, yet one rarely put into practice.

If you learn to prioritize and work on the things that matter and will continue to matter in the future, you will encounter that feeling of urgency less often because you will be prepared for whatever that deadline was. It's a cycle. You get to decide if you're in control of it or trying to catch up to its speed.

Let's close this concept with some practical advice: the way Rory Varden suggests we invest our time in order to multiply it is through automation or procrastination. We can create systems that will save us some time in the future, which therefore returns our time invested in creating them. For example, creating checklists that you can use to make a process smoother, designing systems, constructing templates that make working on a recurring task more effective, making a process automatic, integrating shortcuts, teaching someone to do something that does not require your attention, delegating, and anything else you can think of that means a process will be executed in less time, with less energy and less friction in the future. The second way—procrastination—implies that we can wait to do the things that are not as important (procrastinating on purpose).

For me, planning is an investment of your time, and this is what this book is all about. Planning today uncomplicates tomorrow. Learning is an investment of your time. This is why I have invested so many hours of my time in learning to plan in the most effective way possible.

A SIMPLE PLANNING MAGIC TRICK

So far, I've proposed two methods to define your priorities both of which, I gotta be honest, can become a bit tedious to recreate. I get it. But I've got you covered. It doesn't get simpler than this. I learned this from the YouTuber Nathaniel Drew who talks a lot about mental clarity and the tools to achieve it in his channel. (Let's pretend the two back-to-back YouTube stories are just a coincidence...)

On the left side of his Daily Log, Drew lists what he believes are his most important tasks for the day. Then, on the right side of the page, next to each task he writes in a red pen the "why" for each item, summed up into one or two words. Why am I doing this? What area of my life is it contributing to? Why does this matter?

And that's it. I told you it was simple. I absolutely love this; it's a great way to bring intention to your day and to very clearly be able to see what your priorities are. Of course, if you are not even able to write a why, it most likely means that item should be crossed off. The same goes for any item whose "why" you no longer believe in. The point is to connect action and purpose.

FROM SUNRISE TO SUNSET

Once you have embedded in your brain the three Principles of Productivity on a daily basis—1) honor your commitments, 2) focus on the important tasks, not the menial ones, and 3) stay true to who you are and what works for you—it will be so much easier to plan for and navigate through the day without losing sight of what your end goal is. With that vision in mind, using whatever method suits your needs, you'll recognize what your priorities are. Now, we're ready to rearrange our to-do list and make it sparkle. Let's get into those details I promised earlier, from start to finish.

In his book, Ryder Carroll stresses the importance of a.m. and p.m. Reflections. If you recall, Reflections are the moment where you sit down with nothing but your notebook and favorite pen to meditate on either the day ahead or the day behind. More than a quick check-in on your tasks, it's a check-in on your mental state, your mindset, and your intentions. Are you doing what you said you were going to do? What can you do better? What went great? What can you plan for? These five to ten minutes are the sacred space for clarity that most of us have been missing all of our lives. This reflection is the pause that might completely change the direction of your life. This is where you detach from the clock, the urgency, the unreachable speed life is rushing at and think from an observer's perspective about the course of your day. No judgment. No friction. No distractions. It's just you and your journal, ready to figure out your next best step.

Carroll proposes that your a.m. Reflection is when you plan out your day. Your p.m. Reflection is when you review your day. Pretty obvious; let's move on.

PLANNING OUT YOUR DAY

Open up your notebook, pour yourself a cup of coffee (or tea, we don't discriminate around here), and light up a candle 'cause it's 4:30 a.m. and I'm about to walk you through my ten-minute process for organizing my day, and you're going to do it with me. No seriously, it's 4:30 a.m., 4:32 to be exact, so yeah... Coffee's done, let's do this.

Every morning, I ask myself a series of questions so I can put on paper everything that might be spiraling inside my messy brain. This is how I choose *what* I will do today.

1) WHAT ARE MY PREVIOUS COMMITMENTS?

You most likely knew that one already though, right? Anyway, I'm first looking for the things I had previously scheduled for today, what is due today, what appointments or events I need to show up for, and what tasks I assigned to today, if any. For example, I might have a Pediatrics class at 1 p.m. and a Pharmacology class 5 p.m. and because there's an exam coming, I'm supposed to study Acute Myocardial Infarction sometime today. There, those are the three previous commitments I should follow through on today. Simple.

For this, you'll have to look back at your Monthly Log or your calendar to see what things you had already planned. In my journal, I usually write out the events at the beginning of the

Daily Log, just so they draw my attention. Like I mentioned before, they are also in my digital calendar.

2) WHAT IS THE ONE BIG THING I WANT TO ACCOMPLISH TODAY?

This is life-changing. It's also a pretty common prioritization technique. I'm sure you've heard of picking the three most important tasks for the day and tackling those first and so on. The idea here, however, is to pick *one* thing that you'll accomplish today that will move the needle for you somehow. Pick something that's important, something that's significant, and something that will somehow make a difference in your life. It might be that one previous commitment you made with yourself or something that gets you closer to your goals. It's crucial however to pick only one *big* thing. It can be big in its complexity or the time it takes to accomplish or the impact it might have in your life, but it has to be big somehow. Make sure that if it was the only thing you were to accomplish today, you'd still feel like you earned the day. Just by purposefully choosing what that one big win for the day is, you've brought intention into your day, and therefore, your life.

This is how I personally find the balance between "Embracing my Chronotype" and "Eating the Frog" (doing the hardest, most important task first). By having one big task, I ensure that I will "do the hard thing" sometime today, but I don't force myself to do it first thing in the morning if that's not the best time for me to tackle it. My advice would be to do that thing as early as you see fit, so you avoid procrastinating.

In your journal, this task must stand out from the crowd. It should be staring back at you, unchecked, demanding to get done. Which is why I use a different, much more flamboyant bullet for it. You can accentuate it however you like: highlight it, write it in a different color, create a new symbol for it, write it in bolder larger font, whatever you like, as long as it pops. Just try that out and let me know if you got it done.

3) HOW CAN I MOVE FORWARD IN ANY OF MY GOALS OR PROJECTS TODAY?

I don't go too crazy on this one. Most likely, my One Big Thing is already nudging me closer to my goals. The point here really is to let go of urgency and focus on your own missions. Just take one step forward in one of your projects, no matter how small.

4) WHAT IS EVERYTHING ELSE THAT MY BRAIN THINKS NEEDS TO GET DONE TODAY?

Yeah, just dump all of it on to the page. These are the little things that keep popping up and taxing your attention. Just write them down.

Now, for this, it helps to have a weekly or monthly task list for the things that need to get done soon, but that don't have a due date or specific timeline. For example: clean out messy kitchen drawer, do one load of laundry, call best friend to catch up. All of these things need to get done, but they don't need to get done *today.* So if these were to come up in my morning journaling session, I'd probably add them to my weekly/monthly task list instead of today's list, unless it's something I'd really like to do today. This way I minimize my "today" list.

SHUFFLING TASKS

Now that I have my potential to-do items, I prioritize and reorganize them. This is how I choose *when* I'll be doing each task. Now is when you embrace your chronotype and apply whatever prioritization technique works best for you.

The way I do this in my journal constantly changes. Some days, I'll add numbers so I know what to do first. Other days, I'll assign them to specific time slots in my digital calendar. Sometimes, I'll add a second "One Big Thing" and know that the rest of the tasks can get done whenever. Other days, I'll write times next to the tasks so I know when I'm supposed to start them. Sometimes, I'll create a mini timeline in my Daily Log to organize my day. Other days, I won't organize them because I don't need to. That's the beauty of dot journaling.

The one thing I *always* do, though, is decide if it's something that "has to get done today" or if it's something that "I'd like to get done today, but there is no problem if I totally flake." This is crucial because at any moment of the hectic day, I'll be able to look at my to-do list and know exactly what it is I could or should be doing next, and it totally relieves the pressure from completing every item on my to-do list. It gives me permission to omit tasks, to be imperfect, and therefore to avoid that feeling of underachieving my expectations.

I do have to mention that what works best for me, when it comes to scheduling a hectic day, is calendar blocking. Essentially, this means assigning tasks to a time slot and estimating the amount of time it might take to get them done. But we'll talk more about this in the next chapter.

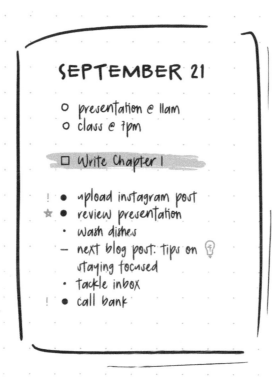

IN REAL TIME

This process is now second nature to me. I don't have think about the questions one-by-one, I just know what it is that I'm looking for. I have other systems in my journal that help me know what I want to be doing that day, which I'll get into in the following chapters, of course. I've done this so many times that it takes no more than ten minutes to plan out my entire day. Of course, I still fail at it every once in a while. I can still have perfectly outlined actions and end up accomplishing nothing throughout the day, but these days are now the exception. I'm still learning to accomplish my goals even better, even more efficiently, but I've come a really long way from rushing through every single task just to have a longer, less meaningful to-do list checked off. And, the sooner you start adding intention to your to-do list, the sooner you will, too.

THE CATCH-ALL EXPERIENCE

Yay! We're done with the first function of the Daily Log! We've successfully planned our day; let's hope the execution goes as smoothly. If it doesn't, feel free to rely on the Ingredients for Productivity Potion to hopefully turn the day around. Once you've organized your day, the second function of the Daily Log kicks into action. It's been so many pages, do you even remember what it was? Just in case: The Daily Log "serves as your catch-all for Rapid Logging your thoughts throughout each day," according to Carroll. This is actually what makes the Daily Log so powerful. Unfortunately, it's something I don't see much about on the internet.

By customizing the bullets and creating your own key, you can turn the Daily Log from a simple to-do list to a one-size-fits-all journal. You can literally write anything in here! Your feelings, thoughts, opinions, journey, memories, what worked, what didn't, what you enjoyed, what you hated, your next million dollar idea, your next terrible idea, all the things you'd like to accomplish someday, a quote that you stumbled upon, notes you don't want to forget, the way your plan turned out, literally, anything. You can write anything and should write everything. This is the place for you to empty your flooding brain. This is where you can store content that you might want to reference in the future. Not just tasks. This is what will transform your journal from a self-drawn planner into a life-changing tool.

Don't waste time looking for the most appropriate Collection or creating a new one to fit your thought, just capture it! Now. On paper. In your Daily Log. You can sort, organize, and reference later... in your p.m. Reflection, ideally. Anyway, I'll talk much more about this—don't worry—because I really believe this is such a powerful tool that most dot journalers don't even know exists. I discovered it not too long ago, myself.

CLOSING THE DAY

One of the beauties of dot journaling is that you get to start every day with a clean slate, literally a new page if you'd like. With your journal, you get to make the choice of what you carry with you into tomorrow. This pause forces you to think and to make a conscious decision about how to handle a task in a split second. You don't even notice it, but you are. You are not a robot tackling tasks that are showing up on your to-do list. You are a person who has goals to prioritize, tasks to eliminate, and an opportunity to grow and be better tomorrow.

In my evening session, I like to look back at my day and interpret what went well, what didn't, what my mood was, and why. Not in a structured manner, not for hours at a time, just a brief pause in my day to breathe in my experiences and grow from them. Once I've reflected. I set my intention for the next day. Not a goal, but an intention, a mindset to carry me through tomorrow. If I'm feeling up for it, I'll go ahead and plan a little for the next day. Again, it takes me no more than ten minutes. It's nighttime. I'm pretty tired and lazy, and I just want fall into bed, usually, so I don't force myself to follow a system. I don't create strict rules. I just try to accept the day so I can find the wins and appreciate them. No matter how hard or wrong the day went, there is something to be grateful about and there is something to be proud of, so notice it, hold on to it, write it down, and let it inspire tomorrow.

CHAPTER 3

Why You Need a Calendar

By now, you must be a bit tired of me blabbering on about productivity... Where's the planning part of this book? Good news, we're here! Unlike the Daily Log, the Monthly and Weekly Logs are where you can actually plan ahead. This is where you take control of your life and get ahead of the current. These spreads are where you can create a bird's eye view of what your near future looks like and steer accordingly. At the essence of both of these spreads is the space under each date for you to assign events, tasks, and projects you wish to accomplish. As opposed to a regular planner though, with dot journaling you can design these spreads to fit all of your needs. Let me show you how.

THE GOOD OLD MONTHLY CALENDAR

This is really a very basic concept you're all familiar with. Most of you might have one hung up in your office or set up stationary on your desk. Because this presentation is so common, a lot of people are used to setting up their calendar (plotting their events, appointments, due dates, birthdays, etc.) at the beginning of the month. Us younger folk might have lost that beautiful tradition since we tend to keep all of our information in an ongoing digital calendar. No breaks. No setting up the new month. Luckily, my high school's planner included monthly calendars, so I learned the value of filling it in every month. This spread, in my opinion, is a very basic one, yet crucial to planning effectively.

SWITCHING TO PROACTIVE MODE

In the productivity realm, there are two basic modes at which you operate: Reactive Mode and Proactive Mode. One will get you by at the expense of your energy, happiness, and satisfaction. The other will *bring you* energy, happiness, and satisfaction. You know how you have that passion project that you wish to tackle someday, but your days are just "too busy"? You just, "don't have the time"? You know that thing you wanted to do, but you've just been "swamped" for the past year? Are you always working late? Never quite caught up? Always surprised by the next appointment on your calendar? If this is your life, let me tell you that you've been living in Reactive Mode. Remember my story in the last chapter about studying for upcoming tests week by week in the first years of med school, and not being able to focus on anything other than the next urgent test? Limited by a one-week timeline? Well, that was me living in Reactive Mode. **Reactive Mode** is when you're always responding to whatever demands life is throwing at you. Life is setting the tone. Life is deciding what you're doing next. Life is in control. **Proactive Mode** is the opposite. It's when you take the wheel, stay on top of everything, and make the choices. It's being aware that you have a project due in three months and are working on it today. It's knowing that daily effort gets you better results than a last-minute cram session. Proactive Mode is how you win at life, it's how you build it, brick by brick. So, how do you make the switch? Create a Monthly Log and *voilà*.

Okay, I may have exaggerated a bit there. You get into Proactive Mode when you are not only planning, but acting ahead. You do this by creating a strategy to achieve whatever goal or deadline you have, and, for the most part, sticking to it. The Monthly Log provides a visual timeline with enough dates for you to create a plan. A week is too short, and a year is too long, but a month is the perfect time for you to look at what you have in the near future and act accordingly. It's what allows you to see that you have a test in the last week of March that you could start incrementally studying for in the first week. It's what makes you aware that your best friend's birthday is coming up and you should start looking for a thoughtful gift. You get the point.

A FORMAT THAT SHINES

You all know how a monthly calendar works. It's mainly composed of, but not limited to, events. I like to use mine sort of like a draft of what my month will look like. I plot my appointments, events, projects, etc. with their corresponding dates and then decide, more or less, when I'll be focusing on those tasks throughout the month. Sort of like this:

MONTHLY CALENDAR

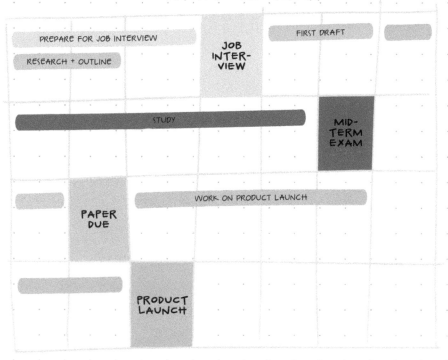

I color coded the events in this example so it's easier to see when I'll be working on each of the projects throughout the month. Like I said, it's a draft. Life happens, and the month probably won't stay like this, but it can provide a very simple guide to fall back on in case things get messy.

You can use whatever format you like for your Monthly Log. I prefer the calendar version because it gives me more space to write in per date. However, on slow months, I love coming back to the original format because the simplicity is so approachable.

The original Monthly Log is composed of two parts: the listed dates and the task list for the month. The idea here is to write down all the things you'd like to get done that month. These complementary headings, in my opinion, are where the magic really happens. For example, you could add the following headings next to your calendar: Book to Read in August, or May's Goals, or April's Work Out Routine, or June's Focus. Just like that, you've automatically added a deadline and created accountability for those things you wanted to do. I'll give you more examples of this later when I get into tracking. For now, try experimenting with different formats and headings in your Monthly Logs.

WEEKLY CALENDARS: YOUR CLEAN SLATE

So far, we've discussed Daily Logs and how to use them to make the most out of your day, and Monthly Logs so you can plan ahead and switch into Proactive Mode. But the pivotal aspect of your planning system is still missing. How do we connect our plans to our daily action? The answer is weekly planning. This is where you take that bird's eye view of the things you wish to accomplish that month and actually assign them a concrete date, place, and time. You turn this hypothetical thing you should do into an actual plan you can follow. And that isn't even the greatest reason why you might want to take some time to plan out the week ahead...

You know that amazing motivation that comes around the New Year? One year is ending, and you're faced with a sea of possibilities for the upcoming one. The slate is wiped clean, the air is filled with potential, your mood is at an all-time high, and your motivation spikes at the thought of all the things you could accomplish this year. That positivity is powerful. January is this ethereal land where everyone is focused on the future and inspired to change their life, but why? Nothing really changes from December 31st to January 1st, besides the date. You're the same, your dreams are the same. Your ambition, however, is through the roof and—if you've got a plan set up—you'll hopefully embrace it to the best of your abilities to achieve one of your goals. Unfortunately, you can't rely on motivation to carry you to the finish line, you need a plan and a system to hold yourself accountable. Nonetheless, it's a powerful weapon. What if you could recreate that feeling of a clean slate? What if you could ignite that motivation on a regular basis, and use it to gain momentum on working towards your goals? What if fresh starts weren't rare at all? I give you: the Weekly Check In.

Your interest is always highest at the beginning of a project when the idea is still fresh. As you get farther away from the start date, motivation fades, and you have to rely on something stronger to keep you going. By breaking down projects or goals into weekly milestones, you create a shorter period of time for you to accomplish that portion of your goal, thus giving you a sense of urgency. You create a clear beginning every single week, thus increasing your motivation to tackle that milestone. The same goes for everything else in your life. When you consider Sunday an unambiguous finish line, you'll have the feeling that each Monday is, in turn, a clean slate. A chance to do things better. By taking the time to check in on the different areas of your life, your goals, and your general responsibilities, you can walk into the following week with a brand new objective and a brand new attitude to tackle whatever challenge comes your way.

Now, wait. If you're thinking "Great! Another complicated thing to add to my planning system," let me just ask you to bear with me for a few minutes. Your check in doesn't have to be complicated, it doesn't have to be sophisticated, it just has to happen. You decide how short and simple you wish to keep it. For illustrative purposes, I'll explain what I do in my normal check in. There are two key components: reflecting on the previous week and planning for the upcoming one.

THE WEEKLY RECAP

The idea behind this section is pretty straight forward, right? A review of how the week went. The concept here is to honestly and objectively reflect on the days that just passed. Why? So you can make better decisions about the week ahead, of course. You'll notice this concept of "pausing" is quite a theme in this book, and that's because I believe that the ability to actively redirect your path is the single most underrated quality of an effective person. Anybody can move stubbornly across their blueprint, but it takes a wise and patient person to reevaluate that plan and course-correct in the moment. These are the people who know how to win. The fastest way out of a maze is by constantly pausing. In the maze of life, more often than not, walking without ever looking back results in getting lost. These snippets of reflection are where I've discovered who I am, what works for me, what I enjoy, and what drains my energy: all of it.

So, you may be wondering: *What do I ask myself?* Well, I wish I had a concrete answer, but it constantly changes. It's not about *what* you're reflecting on, it's about the fact that you are reflecting. I could fill a book with examples of questions that you can ask yourself during reflection. But making these moments too complex will only make them feel like a chore and ensure that you hate these ten minutes of your week. I limit myself to five questions. On occasion, I might even reflect on only a single question. Pick the number that works for you, try that out for a few weeks, and then adjust accordingly.

At times that I'm hyper-focused on my goals, one of my questions might be: "How have you made progress towards your goals this week?" When I'm trying to find happiness in my daily routine, a question might be: "What worked this week? What did not?" When I'm working through a crazy busy schedule, I might ask myself: "What tasks do I have to tackle in the upcoming week? What have I been postponing?" Regardless of what my focus might be, I *always* ask myself, "What were the wins for this week?" This is, by far, my favorite one. There's no greater boost of confidence than flipping through your journal's weekly recaps and reading all the wins you've had over the past few months, all those things you did right.

I'll pick some questions that I'll reflect upon for a few weeks in a row, and when I feel like they need an update, I'll make a new list. Simple.

In case you are interested, these are the questions I generally reflect upon:

1. What were my wins for the week?

2. What worked or didn't work this week?

3. What were the things my brain thinks I need to get done?

4. How am I making progress towards my goals?

5. What do I wish I were doing more of?

TIE IT TOGETHER: SORTING YOUR JOURNAL

Though this might take a few minutes of your time, in the long run, it will simplify your life. When it's time to review:

- Look through your Daily Logs for the week.

- Organize what needs to be organized, file what needs to be filed, and migrate anything to its appropriate collection if necessary.

- Notice what you've accomplished, what's inspired you, and what's made you happy these past days.

- Reflect on the pending tasks.

This migrating and organizing practice has completely changed the way I handle my journal. For example, let's say I came up with an idea for a YouTube video on a random Tuesday. If I were to just leave it there, it would most likely get lost. Instead, on Sunday, when I'm reviewing the week and I stumble upon this idea on Tuesday's Daily Log, I'll create a reference for it in my YouTube Video Ideas Collection.

You can apply this to any piece of information that you wish to keep together. To save you some rewriting time, you can even just write a title for that idea and jot down the page number where you wrote that idea. This allows me to write in my Daily Log without restrictions and to put my thoughts on paper without having to think where they should go. This routine is how I stay on top of many things at once.

Okay, enough about the past. Let's talk about planning for the week ahead.

THE WEEKLY BOARD

Carroll's system jumps from Monthly Logs to Daily Logs without setting up any spreads in between. The internet adapted his method and created the Weekly Log to resemble a traditional planner a bit more. Like I mentioned before, the Weekly Log is a two-page spread that has all seven days of the week set up on it, so you can see everything happening that week at one glance. This is how I started setting up my journal. Until I explored the purpose I wanted dot journaling to serve in my life, and concluded that I needed a place to pour my unfiltered thoughts into more than I needed a tight, planner-like journal. This is the essence of dot journaling and what separates it from a regular planner.

The disadvantage of setting up your two-page weekly spread ahead of time is that you limit the space to write per day. This means that even if you don't notice it, whenever you have a thought, you'll analyze whether it is worth the two lines of space it will take in your already limited ten-line space for that day. Once I stopped hindering the brain dump process of transferring my thoughts to paper, the benefits of journaling oozed into my life. My mind was suddenly clear: I could see what my priorities were and I could see where my attention was going on a regular day. My journal became my second brain. This is why I highly recommend using Daily Logs instead.

There are some aspects of the acclaimed Weekly Log that I did find incredibly useful, however. If you search the internet for these spreads for a minute, you'll see that in addition to setting up the spaces for days, most journalers create sections for other things they wish to track. For example: workouts, meals, tasks,

habits, sleep time, and house chores; the list is endless. You can
create a mini seven-day section to stay on track with any area of
your life, and because it is right next to where you'll be planning
and jotting down your thoughts, you'll be more likely to use it. I
absolutely loved these mini-sections. I initially went crazy with
them, whereas now, I try to keep them as simple as possible.
Like I said, complicating any spread only makes it feel like
another task to tick off. Here are some examples:

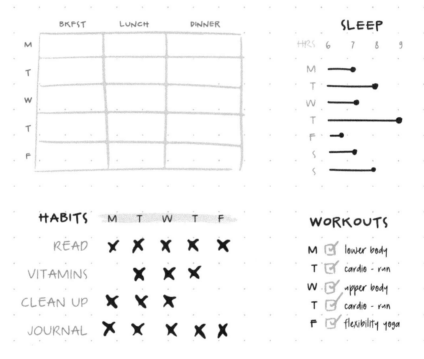

So, when I finally gained enough courage to switch to Daily
Logs, I found myself in a bit of a pickle. How can I keep creating
these mini-sections that keep me on track, yet use Daily Logs
to go about my days? Yeah, I know, no one thinks this is a
problem. But, hey! I am writing a book on planning, so these
things are problems in my mind. Anyway, I came up with The
Weekly Board!

I'm sure you've seen in any rom-com or family movie those hyper-organized parents who have a very beautifully color-coded collection of calendars, lists, bills, and meal plans stuck to their fridge, their "family command center." (I will totally be one of those moms, by the way.) Well, that board is kind of like what the Weekly Board is... hence, the name. To me, the Weekly Board is this space where I can "stick" all the things I need present in my life that specific week. The things I want to track, the goals I want to achieve, the meals I need to plan, the workouts I want to do, or, if it's a slow week, nothing. It changes all the time. The idea is to create a space (mine takes up a maximum of one page) at the beginning of a certain week where I can group all the things I need on my radar. This is my *preview* of the week, where I plan my goals and more or less how I want my week to go. And, guess where I get that information? The Weekly Recap, of course!

Once I have a general idea of how my previous week went, I'll instantly know, more or less. how I want the following one to go. This makes the whole planning process a lot smoother. Again, you can add whatever you want to this command center, but these are the things I generally plan for:

WEEKLY BOARD

A spread to plan ahead for the upcoming week, composed of these four categories to encompass all areas of your life.

GOALS

This is where you write in the goals for this week. These are usually outcomes or milestones for the goals you're currently working on

- ☐ Outcome for top goal
- ☐ Milestone for my project
- ☐ One goal for this week
- ☐ Goal #4

TASKS

This is for the tasks that have to get done or you'd like to get to this week. Can also serve as a braindump section.

- task #1
- Important thing #2
- Can't forget to do this
- Must get done this week
- task #5

EVENTS

This is for an overview of the events that are scheduled for this week.

20 • M	Random Event
21 • T	
22 • W	Something Due
23 • T	
24 • F	Can't Forget
25 • S	Event #4
26 • S	

TRACKERS

This section is for anything you want to track that specific week. Mini 5 or 7 day trackers.

SLEEP   WORKOUTS

HRS 6 7 8 9   M ☑ lower body
                         T ☑ cardio - run
M ——•   W ☑ upper body
T ———•   T ☑ cardio - run
W ——•   F ☑ flexibility yoga
T ———————•
F •   MEALS:
S ——•
S ———•

Feel free to add any other categories and share!

With these four simple categories, I decide what I want my week to look like and what I think I should accomplish during this time.

The reason why I love tracking these things week by week is because it inevitably creates a clean slate. You have to literally recreate a spread for the following week (even if it's composed of the same things). There are no missed habits or undone tasks from the previous week lurking on the adjacent page. This has really allowed me to focus my attention solely on the week at hand, thus reducing my anxiety and locking me into the present moment. If last week was a complete disaster, who cares!? You can start over this week. Leave the planning and sorting-out-your-life for the Weekly Check In session. During the week, focus on doing what you said you were going to do. This little command center serves as your one-page cheat sheet for the upcoming week. By taking just a few minutes to set it up, you'll exponentially increase your focus in the days to come.

So, I "start" my weeks with a Weekly Board. As the days go by, I set up the Daily Logs and close the week off with the Weekly Recap. I don't set up any of these beforehand; I just do it as I go along. Explaining it in detail is complicated—I get it—but putting it into practice is so simple. Have the courage to write whatever thought is crossing your mind without worrying about the wasted space or its correct location on your journal. Instead, take a few minutes a week to sort out your journal. Pick and choose those ideas that might be worth your time and catalog them where they belong, where you'll have quick access to them. Learn about yourself from the notes you took during the week. Come back to your Weekly Board and see if you've accomplished what you said you would this week, then reflect and make adjustments for the upcoming week. This is how you reach your potential.

BONUS: PLANNING FOR PROS

If you wanted more practical details, here we go. Calendar Blocking and Batching are the two strategies that drastically increased my productivity game. If there is any planning advice that you take from this book, take this. I swear, it will change your life.

CALENDAR BLOCKING

Elon Musk created a term called Time Boxing, Bill Gates uses his strategy, Cal Newport calls it Time Blocking, Amy Landino calls it Calendar Blocking, and she's my favorite, so that's why I am using her term in my book. Did you notice the subtle name dropping I just did there? No seriously, these are some highly effective people who are using this technique to plan out their days so, keep reading. You have twenty-four hours in a day. This is where you decide what you'll be doing with each one of them.

The idea of Calendar Blocking is to assign a date and time to a specific task that you want to accomplish, along with an estimate of how much time you wish to or think you might spend on that task. Then, you block that time on the calendar. Kind of like this:

	MON	TUE	WED	THU	FRI	SAT	SUN
6 AM							
7 AM	MORNING ROUTINE	MORNING ROUTINE	MORNING ROUTINE	MORNING ROUTINE	MORNING ROUTINE		
8 AM	ONLINE CLASS	WORK	EDIT YOUTUBE VIDEO	WORK		YOGA CLASS	
9 AM							
10 AM	FILM YOUTUBE VIDEO		CLIENT CALL		CLASS	YOGA CLASS	
11 AM			ONLINE CLASS	MEETING	VIDEO LIVE		CHURCH
12 MD	LUNCH	LUNCH		LUNCH			
1 PM							

This will very quickly make you aware of how you are spending your time and where you can find a few minutes to squeeze in that project you've been wanting to start for so long. This method creates accountability, it creates urgency, and most importantly it defines your hypothetical plans. It's kind of like that encounter with an acquaintance where you run into each other, reminisce about your friendship, and end the conversation with "We should see each other someday." I mean, is that ever going to happen? What if that friend actually says, "You should come out to dinner this Friday"? Now, that's more of a plan. That's exactly what Calendar Blocking does with your tasks.

The first things you might want to block are any recurring tasks. For example, "Work 9-to-5." That's clearly busy time. When you are planning your week, continue with blocking the big tasks that have to get done, and so on. Once you've blocked out all the things you have to do, you'll have a clear picture of what "free" time you have to do the things you *want* to do.

When I hint to my boyfriend that he should use this, he always says that he "hates" having all of his day planned (Calendar Block style, because, I mean, he obviously has a pretty good idea of what he wants to get done on any given day). He argues that as the day goes on and he is not living up to his plan, anxiety starts to build up to a point where he doesn't want to follow the plan anymore. I completely understand... except that it doesn't make sense in my head. Having a general guideline of how you want your day to go will allow you to accomplish more things than if you had no plan at all, even if you didn't accomplish all the things in that plan. So, isn't it better in the end? It's an ongoing argument. Maybe you can help us settle who wins this one...

Anyway, from him I learned that one of the most important skills to embrace in Calendar Blocking is flexibility. You have to able to learn from past experiences how long something might take so you can have a better estimate in the future, and you have to be pliable enough to understand that life happens and, of course, you can't accurately predict a full day. In my life, the blocking system serves as a guideline and a very clear set of instructions on what I would like to be working on at all times. For example, I've completely forgotten to check my calendar today because I've been in the zone for hours, and that's way more valuable than whatever task I had planned for 6 p.m. And, that's okay. This flexibility is important.

> **Magic Trick:** Maybe start with tracking your time for a week, and then start planning ahead. This might help you see what room you have to play with.

DOT JOURNAL OR DIGITAL?

I'm a tech person, so I used to do this on my digital calendar all through college (while still being an avid BuJo user). I would jot down the list of my tasks in my journal and block the time by subjects or themes in my digital calendar. Lately, however, I've experimented with the idea of time blocking small chunks in my journal. For example, I block only my after-work hours (4-9). There are, for sure, many ways in which you can do this in your notebook, so I'll just share some examples with you. Remember to do whatever works for you!

Magic Trick: The way I like to block my time is by "project." For example: today, 9-12, work on JPM CH4. The subtasks for that are in my journal: edit, make a list of the illustrations, add terms to glossary, copy final outline, etc.

BATCHING

Batching is pretty much what it sounds like: combining similar tasks into a batch and then working on them for a dedicated period of time. For example, when I make YouTube videos, instead of filming twice a week, I'll batch Filming Video 1 and Video 2, sit down, and record them back to back. This means that instead of setting everything up twice, I only have to do it once a week, thus saving me a lot of time and effort. Another example could be taking the pictures for my Instagram. It's much more effective to shoot, edit, and caption a bunch of pictures at once than to go through that process every day.

Batching tasks doesn't just save you time. There is a certain flow or mindset that you get into when you have to work on different tasks. For instance, the mindset I'm in when I have to study (analytical, slow paced, detail oriented) is very different than the mindset I'm in when I'm filming (creative, fast paced, extroverted), and that's different than the mindset I'm in when I'm cleaning my house (mechanical, unfocused).

The workflow is different as well. Switching from one kind of activity to another requires a lot of energy, and getting into the flow of that activity takes a lot of time, so by batching, you are maximizing your efforts and thus being more effective. This also means that you'll spend more time working on a certain kind of activity which increases the likelihood of getting into a deep, productive mode. In his book *Deep Work*, Cal Newport explains the concept of attention residue. This theory states that "when you switch from some Task A to another, Task B, your attention doesn't immediately follow—a residue of your attention remains stuck thinking about the original task." This results in poor performance on Task B. Batching minimizes this attention residue by reducing the number of times we switch tasks.

When you are planning the upcoming week, ask yourself: *What similar tasks can I batch and assign to a specific day in the calendar?*

LITTLE THINGS, BIG IMPACT

I think this may be one of the most important chapters of this book when it comes to time management and efficiency. Proactive monthly planning, the Weekly Check In session, Calendar Blocking, and batching are the core strategies that sky-rocketed my productivity. They're also, unfortunately, the easiest to stop doing. It's so clear to me how my productivity plummets whenever I stop applying these things. There is much more to productivity and planning, hence the rest of the book... but these strategies are crucial to staying on top of your life. Combining The Weekly Check In with batching tasks and Calendar Blocking can have a massive impact in what you accomplish. This is how I get my life together. And if you give them a solid try, they might do the same for you.

PART II

Let's Add Some Magic

CHAPTER 4

Tips and Tricks to Make It Yours

O ne of the greatest complaints I hear about planning with an analog system is that it's not as efficient as a digital one. Being the efficiency maniac that I am, I needed to find a way to make my journal more dynamic. Locating a spread had to be easier than scanning through sixty pages of my messy handwriting. So, over the years I've learned—and come up with—a few tricks to level up my journaling game. These are my favorite ones.

STAYING ORGANIZED

My favorite digital tool ever is the search bar. With a few keystrokes, you can open any document in your computer in seconds. Unfortunately, the Index in your notebook is not a good enough substitute for that. The magic and joy of using a dot journal comes when it's just as easy to find something you wrote ages ago. Let's find out how.

THE INDEX

I wish I had cracked this for you guys. Unfortunately, after seven notebooks, I have not yet figured out the best way to set up your index. In the past, I've tried multiple indexes for different categories. I've tried color coding. I've tried highlighting the spreads I am constantly coming back to. None of these methods have proved themselves to be efficient enough to find things quickly. The only thing that I've found the index to be indispensable for is finding old collections in the journals I'm no longer using. I suggest you play around and find what works best for you. I, instead, do the following.

MAGIC TRICKS

1. LABEL THE FORE EDGE

In case you don't know what that means—since I had to google it for this title—it's the vertical edge of the book opposite to the spine, where the pages aren't connected. Anyway, find your favorite way to color or label this edge of your journal so that you can identify where the pages are at a glance. I'll show you how in a few pages.

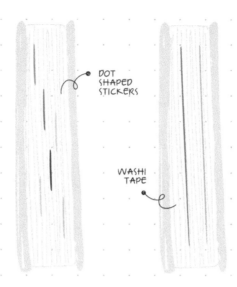

DOT
SHAPED
STICKERS

WASHI
TAPE

2. BLANK FIRST PAGES

When you're setting it up, leave a few blank pages at the
beginning of the notebook in case you come up with any spreads
that relate to multiple months or that you need to reference
easily. For example, this March, I decided to start tracking my
Instagram engagement again. This is something I'd be filling
in on a weekly basis, so by including it at the beginning of my
journal, it's much easier to find than having it randomly placed
after March's spreads. The blank pages are great for trackers
that apply to the entire year.

3. TRACK BY MONTH

You'll notice, if you haven't already, that I organize my life by
months. I choose my goals by month, the habits I'm going to
track by month, the events I need to stay aware of by month, etc.
So, when setting up your month, try to group all the trackers
and spreads relevant to that month before you start writing

your Weekly or Daily Logs. This way, you only have to label the beginning of the month, and the rest will be easy to access.

4. CODE

Categorize and color code as much as necessary and as little as possible. What I mean is, don't overcomplicate your system. Find the categories that you constantly need to visualize in your life, and only color code those. For example, categorize by classes, kids, areas of your life, jobs, or projects. Not all of them at the same time. You don't want your key to be overcomplicated because you won't rely on it. The point of color coding is to be able recognize what category anything belongs to at a glance.

5. USE WEEK NUMBERS

Trust me. If you learn to look at the calendar in terms of week numbers, you'll be so much more aware of what you're supposed to be doing that week. You'll be able to plan in week-blocks and get some consistency across all your planners.

MUST-HAVE SPREADS

1. GRID MAP

This spread is basically a breakdown of the number of rows and columns *your* journal contains, along with some of the most common ways of dividing the page. It's kind of hard to explain, so let me just show you.

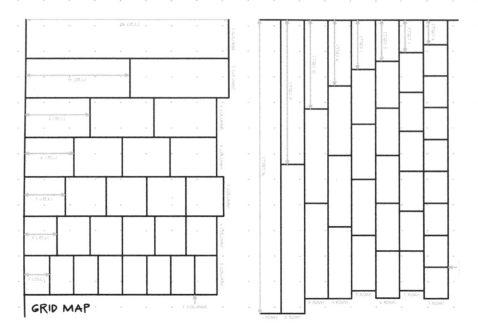

GRID MAP

This shows you exactly how many "cells" you need to count in order to break down your page. This will vary depending on the size of your notebook. It's super useful when creating new spreads and saves you a bunch of time, especially if you're a beginner. I suggest that you create one to fit the cells in your journal.

2. BIRD'S EYE VIEW

Part of the wonder of this system is being able to see the big picture. There are two spreads that are made for that. A simple calendar of the entire year and the Future Log. Or, a combination of the two. The yearly calendar is a spread I find myself turning to constantly. If you're doing your planning, it's so much easier to turn to the first page of your notebook and look for a date than to drop everything, open your device, and search for the calendar. The Future Log is especially essential if you use only your journal for planning your entire life. You'll need a place to capture dates of events that are happening in a few months.

> **Magic Trick:** If you don't want to waste hours of your time rewriting 1-30 twelve times, just print a yearly calendar and paste it to your journal!

3. SOMETIME SOON LIST

I tried to limit the number of specific spreads I'm encouraging you to create in your journal, but this one is a must-have. The idea of a Sometime Soon List is to capture the mini-projects, large tasks, goals, and ideas you would like to get to *sometime soon*. I swear that this is life changing. A lot of the time, these ideas seem too big to incorporate into the next day's to-do list, but too small to be projects of their own; thus, they get lost in your journal and are never executed. I propose you group them into a Sometime Soon list.

Once a week, take the time to look at this list and choose (if you can) one thing you can tackle. For example, let's say this week I decided I was going to work on my website and in my Sometime Soon List I have a cumbersome task for my website I need to take care of. This week seems like the perfect time to do so. These can also be things you've been wanting to do. For example, my list at the moment includes "take a creativity challenge." Whenever I'm less busy and a bit more motivated I'll include that in my plans for the week. Usually, I go through this list every Sunday as I'm planning the week ahead. Trust me. Try it out, you'll never go back.

Magic Trick: I have a section in this list called "Next on My BuJo" which has ideas of spreads I'd like to create, things I'd like to track or pursue, and formats I'd like to try. Stuff like that. Super fun.

4. WHATEVER YOU NEED

I'm serious! Create a spread for whatever *you* need. These are the most important ones because they're how you'll really reap the benefits of this method. Track what needs awareness in your life, so you can notice your patterns and tweak them to your preference. Find what needs attention. This is yours, for *you* to grow with.

For example, when I was having trouble sticking to a bedtime, I created a sleep tracker. When I wanted to read more, I created a tracker for the books I read during the year. When I needed to unscramble my brain, I journaled. When I wanted to lose weight, I tracked my progress. And so on. You'll be surprised at the impact that tracking something has on your behavior. By dedicating the time and energy to tracking these patterns, you're actively working on improving them, and you'll have the visual feedback you need to make the right adjustments. Take it slow. Don't over-track your life. Instead, find what needs love and pour it into the pages of your journal.

BONUS: YOUR IDEAL SELF

I guess these are not essential, yet, I believe, quite powerful. Your journal shouldn't just be this boring rigorous monotonous productivity tool. It is so much more. It's your second brain. It's your dreams. It's your potential. Which is why I like to include my "Ideal Self Spreads," for a lack of a better name. These are collections of what my ideal life looks like at this moment. For example, my daily routines, my self-care ideas, a description of my goals, what I need to have a balanced life, my values, and my dreams. Manifest these things into your journal and track the reality to see where you stand. Let these pages be a guide to what you want your life to look like. Let them inspire you. In my opinion, these are what make your journal unique. Ideal Self Spreads probably aren't everyone's cup of tea, and that's okay. The idea is to be able to see what your life looks like throughout the years in terms of what you value, what you express, and who you are.

MY FAVORITE HACKS

Finally, a compilation of some of my favorite hacks to make your life easier and level up your journal. There are tons of ideas on the internet. These are the ones I've found the most useful.

1. WASHI TAPE AND DOT STICKERS ON THE FORE EDGE

Remember how we talked about labeling the fore edge of the journal to make spreads easier to find? Well, this is the easiest way to do it. Take a string of washi tape and paste half of it at the edge of the page, then fold the remaining half towards the back of the page. There! Now you've got a clear, easy-to-find color coded edge of the page. My favorite way to do this, however, is with circle-shaped stickers. I buy white ones and color them in with a color that matches my spread. This way, I'll remember what spread each label belongs to. You could also buy the already colored circle stickers and create a color code for categories of spreads. This is more or less what that looks like:

1. COLOR WHITE DOT SHAPED STICKER
2. PASTE HALF OF THE STICKER ON THE EDGE OF THE PAGE
3. FOLD BACKWARDS

Magic Trick: Write titles for your spreads so you can easily identify them.

This is a game changer and, by far, my favorite dot journaling hack of all time. This is what makes my collections so easy to access and my workflow so frictionless.

2. REFERENCE SYMBOL

This is an essential part of my system, and one of the most used icons in my key. It means "found on." When I'm planning, especially for projects, I need to be able to access information that is either in another page on my journal or somewhere on my computer. To solve this issue—and avoid using valuable brainpower to remember where that is—I created a symbol that indicates where it's found. For example, let's say I came up with an idea for a video and I randomly described the details on a Daily Log on page 56, On my Video Ideas List, I might add the title and then ▷ 56, meaning that the rest of the information is found on that page.

3. THREAD THE PAGES

Can't picture my journal without this. The idea of threading is to easily reference where a Collection continues. Let's say you started a "Books to Read" list on page four, but you've filled the entire page, so on page 29, you continue the collection with more titles. This way, you don't have to worry about leaving blank pages in case you run out of space. Threading looks something like this:

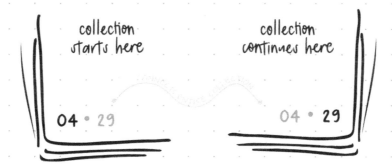

MORE WAYS TO GET CREATIVE

I've already mentioned my most-used journal planning hacks. The rest are some additional hacks I found worthy of being mentioned in this book, in no particular order. Enjoy.

- Use white out tape instead of liquid Wite-Out. This allows you cover your mistakes and write over them immediately, and it's just less messy.

- Paste a bunch of Post-it notes on the last page of your journal; this way, you'll always have them on hand.

- Use colored stickers or Post-its to highlight a bullet in your Daily Log.

- Fold a page in half to create a divider in your journal.

- If your journal doesn't already have one, paste an envelope to the inside cover. This will be more useful than you imagine.

- Use flags (small Post-its) to reference spreads you'll need temporarily. For permanent references, the washi tape or dot stickers are better, as flags might get ruined when you carry your journal around. I love doing this for the spreads I need to fill in consistently throughout a month, this way I never forget to fill in my trackers.

- Loop the elastic around the top left corner of your notebook so you can carry around a pen.

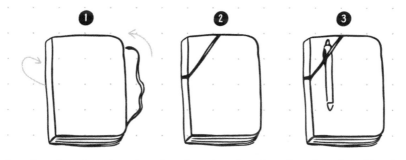

- Use stencils to draw boxes. You don't have to count; you barely have to think, just trace!

- Cover a mistake with a black box and write on it with a white pen; it makes it look like you did it on purpose.

- Attach Post-its to a spread so you can reuse the layouts. A great example is a meal planning layout!

- Print graph paper so you don't have to draw million little boxes for your trackers. Or, buy a grid notebook instead of a dotted one.

These tricks have really changed the way I look at my journal and how efficiently I can use it. If you have any other hacks, I'd love to hear them. Share them with **#planningmagic** so I can learn from you as well!

CHAPTER 5

A Pop of Color

While the Bullet Journal originated as a method for planning, the community turned it into a form of creative journaling. If you look around the internet, you'll mainly find inspiration for beautifully designed spreads, pages full of color, drawings, tape, pictures along with the corresponding Monday–Sunday labels, and tiny spaces for to-do lists and journaling. While that's great for inspiration, it can be very daunting if you're a beginner. Your journal doesn't have to look like that. Remember that this is a tool to better your productivity, help you achieve your goals, and most importantly, find calm. I believe in finding the balance between the aesthetic and functional aspect of your journal. However, you are free to do as you please.

Your notebook should be a safe space to express whatever is going through your mind. Some people need more art, others need more structure, and some of us need them both. In this chapter, I'll attempt to introduce you to this creative world within dot journaling and give you a few tips that will come in handy during your planning sessions. You don't need to do any of this to "effectively" journal, so if decorating is not your thing at all, feel free to skip to the next chapter.

DO "WASTE" TIME DECORATING

It's okay. More than okay, there is value in this. "Decorating" your planner is about a lot more than just making it look pretty. Part of the reason I fell in love with dot journaling is that it was introduced to me at a period in my life when I was in a creative rut. My artistic self was nowhere to be found. I couldn't stop myself from thinking logically. That's what spending eighteen hours a day learning medical facts does to you, I guess. Anyway, journaling became my ten-minute creative outlet, and I think that's why a lot of other people enjoy it so much, too.

If you have an ounce of creativity within you—and I believe we all do—this is a simple way to let it run free. When you're using your creative brain, you're forced to invest all your attention on the task at hand because your brain needs to make connections; it needs to flow. Zoning in on your focus forces you to slow down and to plan with intention and love. That sounds cheesy, but I mean it. It allows you to really pay attention to what you're doing. I believe that the creative mindset you need to set up a spread and choose decorations spills over into your plans. When you're exploring ideas and thinking outside the box in your journal, you're bound to do the same when it comes to organizing your schedule, planning your days, and solving problems. This inevitably influences the way you find solutions, even if you barely notice it.

Regardless of this, let's just be real and accept that aesthetics are motivating. I mean, your surroundings influence you, and so can the places where you plan. Remember that these pages are what you're going to be staring at frequently, so you want them to be pleasurable to look at. You want them to be inspiring, calming, motivating, and easy to understand. Plus, there's a little bit of pride that you feel when you look at a nice spread you created, and who doesn't need that small dose of motivation when you're about to get things done? In my opinion, what you wrote matters much more than how your page looks, because in the end, it's about how you are living your life. But, if looking at a beautiful page you created makes it even one percent easier for you to achieve your goals, then do it. It's worth it.

For me, creative journaling is a way to slow down, enjoy the process of planning, and get me excited about the things I want to do. These planning/crafting sessions are cathartic. They are a ritual of pause that I want in my life. As long as decorating doesn't keep you from taking action, it's not a waste of time.

JOURNALING STYLES

There are so many to choose from! You could start with a minimalist approach: simple fonts, minimal decorations, and practically no color. You could go slightly decorative, where you have fun with the titles and color schemes. You could choose doodle style, where you pick a theme and draw decorations around the spreads. Or maybe pick scrapbook style, where you collage papers, stickers, pictures, and whatever you can think of. If you're an artist, you can do sketchbook style, where the drawings are the center of attention and the planning surrounds the images. Or, you could do what I do and mix it all up! You don't have to choose a style, you don't have to stick to rules, just do you. Do whatever you feel like doing in the moment. You'll realize it's usually what you need a dose of. Remember to have fun and indulge in creative expression. Feel free to do whatever you want, even if you think it looks horrible. Because this is for you and it should represent where you're at. Just don't let any of this ruin your plans, it's supposed to be a functional system, so find what works for you.

NIFTY JOURNALING TOOLS

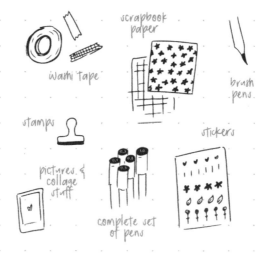

Let me just say you don't need any of these supplies for effective dot journaling. However, they'll come in handy if you want to decorate your journal. My advice is, if you're a beginner, to start with one or two items and stick to them for a while. Get creative!

JUST A POP

Instead of providing you inspiration, which you can find online in less than a minute, I thought I'd give you a few tips on decorating your spreads. More specifically: doing it fast. The idea is to find the way to add a quick spark to your journal when you're too busy to spend hours working on it. Like I said, it's about finding the balance between function and form.

- This is a fairly obvious one: use pencil first. It seems like a waste of time, but it'll save you lots of energy and frustration, trust me.

- Add pops of color. Highlight some of the things that need your attention. Trace numbers, dates, bullets, or symbols with a color. Add a few random blobs of that color to the page. That will bring the whole spread together.

- If you need to write a lot, but want a "pretty-looking" page, just add a big cool title and a border, and you're good to go.

- Use washi tape for titles. It'll automatically elevate your spread and save you lots of time.

- When in doubt and on a time crunch, just use stamps! There are so many styles for you to pick from, but *one* alphabet will do the trick. This is a great, effortless way to add style to your spreads immediately. And it's one of my absolute favorites.

- Cheat on your lettering! I know, this sounds bad. Trust me, though; this is how I started. All you have to do is write out a word in cursive (leave some space between the letters) and thicken the down strokes. Kind of like this:

1. WRITE DESIRED WORD. LEAVE SPACE BETWEEN THE LETTERS

2. CREATE A SECOND LINE ONLY ON THE DOWNSTROKES

3. FILL IN THE GAPS !

- Draw what you see! This is a creative way to add character to your journal. I especially love doing this on my Daily Logs or journal entries. Just add a quick sketch of some of the things you see. For example, your coffee cup, the pens you're using, your glasses, a plant that's in front of you, or the scenery you're staring at (alright, that one's a bit more complicated, but you get the point). It's also really cool to look back at these tiny glimpses of your daily life. Plus, you get to practice your drawing skills.

- If you can't draw at all, find yourself a good set of icon stamps. My favorite way to use them is to color in a small blob and stamp over it. You can use this to represent events or memories or just to decorate.

- If you hate lettering, use stickers. You can find them in pretty much any stationery store. Look for the stickers with the months, days, or even holidays in cool fonts. This saves you time and effortlessly adds cuteness to your journal.

- Use thought bubbles to draw attention to notes!

- Add quotes on random pages! Fill a full page with one quote. This adds variety and also expresses your mindset at the moment. Quotes are a great way to fill empty space.

YOU CAN EVEN COLOR THEM IN TO ADD LIFE TO YOUR JOURNAL

- If you're going to create a full decorative spread, design a color scheme. This will save you from making mistakes, and it'll add cohesiveness and spark to your pages.

COLOR SCHEME

- Paste random pictures on random spreads. I know this sounds weird. One overthinking human like me would think that the picture had to represent what you're writing about. And that's fine. But, it doesn't! I love adding random pictures, especially on journal entries for color effect.

- If you want to go the extra mile, draw on the picture. Add a frame, maybe a drop shadow, or add tiny doodles or patterns to elevate the aesthetic.

Finally, find inspiration online! There's an entire world out there. Become a part of it, create, inspire, share, and win the dot journaling game. Most creators have a specific style they share online, so I would advise picking your favorite styles. Get out of your comfort zone and find all sorts of inspiration! It's okay to start by copying spreads (if you share, make sure to credit whose spread yours is based on). This is how you'll become confident with the technique and start creating your own style. The fact that you feel proud of the spread you created will give you a confidence boost to go after your plans as well. Most importantly, enjoy the process—that's where you find calm and small doses of happiness.

CREATIVE HACKS

I believe the following hacks have allowed me to stay creative on my journey. If you want this creative outlet to be part of your life, it has to be easy. These tips make my life easier and encourage me to decorate my journal. They will surely do the same for you!

GLUE FIASCO

Use glue tape. If you want to add pictures and papers, pasting is your worst enemy...until you find glue tape. It's basically roll-on tape that is actually glue and a completely mess-free way to scrapbook your journal.

THE TOOLS MATTER

Stick to your favorite pens. Especially when it comes to lettering, just find some that work for you and stick to those until you've mastered the technique. Also, while I'm on this topic, do yourself the favor of picking a nice smooth pen for you to do all the writing with. It's worth it.

PEN PACK

Use different sized black pens. I'm sure you've seen the pack of Micron or Staedtler pens online, this is what I mean. They include sizes that vary from 0.1 to 1 mm. When you're creating spreads, this just elevates the aesthetic so much. You can use one thickness for lines and another for numbers, doodles, or titles. It'll just make the spreads so much neater and easy to look at.

SKETCH, SKETCH, SKETCH

Have a pen test page. Trust me, you need it. Preferably not the last page of your journal, since you might run into this one too often and it'll not be a pretty page to look at. You need a space in your journal where you can try out pens, colors, and color schemes. This will save you so much effort in the long run and make it easier to decorate your journal on the go.

THE PICTURE TRICK

Print a bunch of pictures and carry them in your notebook's pocket. This is what allowed me to add scrapbook style spreads to my journal. I always wanted to create them, but never really found the time or energy to look for pictures, print them, cut them out, and add them to my journal. This was way too much work. So, one weekend, I poured myself a glass of wine, turned on *Friends*, plunged into Pinterest, found like one hundred pictures I liked—random, pretty kind of pictures—printed them, cut them out, and now I carry them in my journal. This and the glue tape allow me to randomly and quickly add pictures to my spread for a scrapbook pop of color effect. Trust me, you need this!

Hopefully, some of these hacks are worth keeping in your back pocket. Get creative and definitely share any tips you have with me! We're all learning here.

To share, use this hashtag: **#planningmagic**

CHAPTER 6
The Eye of the Hurricane

There is no denying that journaling is a powerful tool. It's on us to find how it plays into our lives. We all have the ability to "keep it all together." All you need is to discover how.

> *"Think about the eye of a hurricane. No matter how intense the storm or what's swept up in its gale-force winds, that calm blue center is always there. We all have this quiet center within us."*
>
> *—George Mumford, The Mindful Athlete*

DOT JOURNALING FOR CALM

Although the dot journal is perceived as a productivity tool, the psychological and mindset benefits of this practice are immense. The facts are that, one, you have everything in one notebook, and two, you've prepared for the future, which will significantly increase your peace of mind. You no longer have to wonder where that idea went, what you wanted to buy at the supermarket, or if you've forgotten an appointment because it's all in your journal. Safe and sound. Yet, there are other aspects of this practice that contribute to a serene state of mind.

Think about your average day. What are the little things that are constantly distracting you? Take big life problems out of the equation for a moment; we'll get to those later. What are the small thoughts that hijack your attention, that your brain keeps shoving to the front row, screaming at you to deal with them? These recurring thoughts that your mind is actively trying not to forget is what David Allen calls "open loops" in his book *Getting Things Done*. He defines them as "anything that does not belong where it is, the way it is." For example: an unfinished task, a piece of information that needs to be captured, an emotion that needs to be dealt with, a memory you don't want to forget, etc. Cal Newport further supports this claim in his book *Deep Work* with the "Zeigarnik effect" which is the "ability of unfinished tasks to dominate your attention." Regardless of what you want to call it, the fact that these thoughts exist in *your* mind is undeniable and, while it may not be obvious, they're hindering your focus, cluttering your brain, and destroying your peace of mind. How can your mind reach peak performance if it's constantly being disturbed by these floating thoughts?

Journal planning offers a simple solution to that problem: **capture your thoughts.** There and then, write it down. In your Daily Log. Just write it down. This habit of capturing your thoughts immediately is one of the most valuable practices I've ever adopted, and I didn't succeed at it until I started dot journaling. The lack of friction between the thought and writing it down—and the free format—makes this the ultimate tool to dump your thoughts as they happen. The organizing, sorting, and actually dealing with these comes later, as we've previously discussed.

There is a caveat to this magic trick, though. In order for your mind to actually let go of the thought, you need to capture it in a system your brain trusts. What I mean is, a place that your brain knows you'll come back to and that you'll revisit when needed so that therefore, that thought or task won't actually be forgotten. What better place for your brain to trust than the little, roughly two hundred-page notebook where your entire life is stored? If you've built the habit of *using* your journal, your brain will believe that it's a safe place to store your thoughts. This means that if you've just started dot journaling or you're not used to coming back to your journal yet, you might not see the benefits of dumping your thoughts onto the page because it won't actually free your mind. Give it some time and trust the process. You won't regret it.

Speaking of freeing your mind, there's another powerful spread that is essential to Bullet Journaling: **The Brain Dump.** There are many types, but the idea is to list whatever is going through your brain. Usually, these are tasks pertaining to a specific subject. For example: "Things to do this weekend," "Things to buy at the supermarket," or "What to do on vacation." Or, my personal favorite, just a good old let's-free-our-mind brain dump where you empty into list form whatever tasks, thoughts, or notes are going through your brain. This takes the pressure off of having to write in prose and making sense of what you're saying. It allows you to treat every item as an open loop. The idea is to give those thoughts a safe place that you can come back to and sort later. The simple action of capturing them on paper allows your brain to let them go and focus on whatever is in front of you. It'll feel like a load off your shoulders.

In classic GTD (Getting Things Done) style, this can serve as your **Task Inbox.** This is basically a list where you collect those little not-so-important tasks in order to free your mind. This is crucial if you want to stay on top of everything. After the tasks have been captured, you can go through them and migrate them to their appropriate list, where you'll be able to access them when necessary. Or, you can assign them a date and time to make sure you get them done. The idea is to have a place to drop your open loops, so that they can be handled later.

Aside from capturing those ideas and tasks, dot journaling allows you to organize them. By planning ahead, you can *see* that whatever you have to do is possible. You can rest peacefully, knowing that you've planned a solution to your problems.

LONG-FORM JOURNALING

When you hear the word "journaling," what do you think of? Recording, thinking, writing, prose. Right? How much of that do you do when dot journaling? At least on the internet, most of what you see is plans, charts, graphs, calendars. I get it. If you write entire paragraphs on your deepest thoughts you might be reluctant to share them online. This, however, has caused many beginners to believe that the BuJo system is purely for planning. It's not. One of the reasons why this method is so rich is because of the ability for you to *journal* your thoughts, whether that means recording them in a sentence, a paragraph, or three pages. This practice is what will help you discover who you are and how you function.

What I mean by long-form journaling is the uninterrupted recording of your thoughts, emotions, goals and/or ideas. Usually through writing prose, without restraint, for a few paragraphs. The simplicity with which you can empty your brain by transferring it to paper is what makes this method so approachable. You don't have to be a writer; you don't even have to understand what it is you are writing. You just have to take it out of your brain and onto paper. Why? Precisely for that, so that it is out of your brain.

Whereas my mom taught me about mindset in a very powerful, loud kind of way, her sister—my aunt—taught be about mindset in a calm, completely in-control kind of way. Which, if you knew them, you'd think is pretty ironic. When I was "little," I practiced horseback riding, and I specifically remember a very important moment in my life during those years. I was about to go into the arena, and I remember sitting tall on my high horse about to throw up, completely overcome with nerves and a fair dose of self-doubt. Right before I had to go in, my aunt approached me. She could see the lack of confidence in my face, I assume, because she slowly pet my horse, looked into my eyes, and said "There are only two types of players—those who keep their nerves under control and win championships, and those who don't. ¿Cuál vas a ser tú? (Which one will you be?)"

More than teaching me how to control my nerves, she taught me the importance of leaving all that noise outside the ring. By the way, she did tell me it was a quote by Harry Vardon—which she heard in the movie *The Greatest Game Ever Played*—that part of the story just never seemed to stick in my brain. As I grew up, it was no longer nerves that I needed to tame, but anxiety, and that's a much bigger monster. The uneasiness, the stressors, the overthinking—it's not a great place to be in. Throughout medical school, I had to learn all over again how to escape that headspace. Better yet, how to deal with it. That's right about when I discovered journaling. Through writing my thoughts, I was able to leave them outside of my performance (my day-to-day life). I could always come back to them, but now they lived outside of my mind, on paper. The great thing is that this isn't just limited to anxiety. You can journal when you're feeling overwhelmed, busy, irritated, nervous, unfocused, jumpy, happy, anything. Thoughts have less power over you if you put them on paper because you don't have to think about them anymore. You can take back that control and win championships.

Journaling is a form of meditation. It allows you to find that calm center and lets everything else cram into your notebook instead of your mind. You are not your thoughts. They are just that, thoughts. Just like with an appointment or an idea that you'll capture immediately, they also need a place to go. A place for safekeeping or for letting them go. Journaling is just the manner with which you can process them, whether that means diving deeper in order to understand them or putting them on paper so you can let them go. Giving yourself the permission to express candidly whatever it is you're thinking—even the bad things, even the angry thoughts, even the ungrateful ones—is freeing. Isn't it better they live in a notebook than in your mind, clouding your judgement, affecting your mood, and distracting your brain? The notebook and pen compose this distance you need to observe your thoughts instead of dwelling in them. To reach clarity. And what is calm if not clarity? What is calm if not understanding? What is calm if not acceptance?

There are many ways to unload your thoughts. Capturing them immediately, like we talked about before, works great for small, straightforward ones. However, how do we unload the big things? The complex ones? The stories we want to forget? The stories we want to remember? Well, it's up to you. Find what works for you. My personal favorite is Stream of Consciousness Journaling. This concept was introduced by William James in his book *Principles of Psychology.* In essence, Stream of Consciousness Journaling is writing your thoughts in a continuous flow. Uninterrupted, unstructured, unbiased. Just writing whatever is going through your mind, whether it makes sense or not. Since James, there have been many adaptations of the technique. It's become a literary style. A form of it is used in psychological therapy. The author Julia Cameron ritualized it into what she calls "Morning Pages," the practice of writing your thoughts for three pages every morning in order to free your mind of creative blocks. The wonder of this method comes from the fact that you don't know what it is you are going to write until you write it. There is no plan or topic you want to think about, there is just emptying whatever thoughts naturally flow through your mind at that specific time. Multiple times, I have figured out what I'm actually thinking or feeling through journaling. That's a powerful tool to have at your disposal.

Other ways to journal your thoughts might be through creative writing, poetry, daily journaling, drawing, keeping one of the million kinds of journals—art, creative, dream, vision, gratitude, prayer, or deep thoughts journals—or even embracing our inner third grader and keeping a diary. Or, a combination of all of them. It doesn't matter what your vessel is, what matters is that you use it on a regular basis to create order from chaos.

THE PERFECT PARTNERSHIP

It makes sense to keep your "long form journaling" notebook separate from your dot journal, especially if it's a deep thoughts journal or a diary. That's okay and totally up to you. What matters the most really is that it's a safe place for you to pour your soul into without being scared you might be judged or hurt someone else's feelings. Just like you need to trust your system to empty your bugging thoughts, you need to trust that your notebook is a safe place in order for you to truly be honest with yourself.

That being said, not everything we journal about is a deep emotional secret. Sometimes, you really just need to sort out your mind, and you should be able to use your journal for that, simply because it's more practical. It's what will be with you everywhere, and it's what already contains your brain, thoughts, and ideas, so it should be easy to maybe write a paragraph or two if you need a few minutes of meditation. This is another reason why I like using Daily Logs. If there is a pressing problem or something I'm anxious about, or I need to make a decision,

I might journal a few paragraphs right there in my journal in order to clear my head.

If you want to incorporate journaling into your dot journal, you can use Carroll's method. He creates a "note" bullet for the thought he wants to journal on. For example: *I'm feeling particularly moody today.* Then, he'll continue with his day as usual and add bullets and tasks as necessary. Once he finds a few minutes to empty his mind, in the next empty line of his Daily Log, he will start to journal about why he might be feeling moody. He will then turn the bullet from a note one to a "plus" sign, to represent that there is *more* on this thought in his journal. I think this is an amazing idea and love the practicality of it. Here's what that looks like.

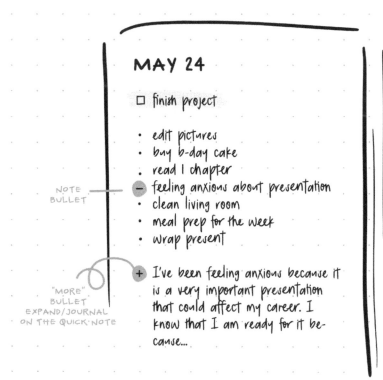

MAY 24

☐ finish project

- edit pictures
- buy b-day cake
- read 1 chapter
- — feeling anxious about presentation   NOTE BULLET
- clean living room
- meal prep for the week
- wrap present

+ I've been feeling anxious because it   "MORE" BULLET
is a very important presentation   EXPAND/JOURNAL
that could affect my career. I   ON THE QUICK NOTE
know that I am ready for it be-
cause...

When I want to dig deeper into my thoughts and emotions, though, I find peace in having a separate journal—probably because I share my journal online. What I'll do is write the prompt in my Daily Log as it crosses my mind. When I find the time, I'll write about it in my private journal, sometimes as part of my night routine. Having a consistent journaling practice is what allows me to keep a cloudless mind and stay focused on what matters.

Where and how you journal doesn't matter. What matters is that you find the way in which the BuJo and long-form journaling create the perfect partnership for you. Use your journal for more than just planning. Let it be a glimpse of you, honest and observant. What matters is that you have a method to empty your brain and place yourself back in the eye of the hurricane. Leave all the tangled mess outside and find calm though journaling. Whenever you need it. However you need it.

CHAPTER 7

Dot Journaling for the Digital Age

Who are we kidding...we're all borderline dependent on our phones. Who can even live without little reminders beeping to make sure you get stuff done? I totally agree. The digital world is essential in the productivity game. But so is the analog one. Most people will force themselves to choose one or the other. I, on the other hand, believe that by merging these tools, you can create the perfect productivity system tailored to you. The digital and analog systems each have their own advantages and disadvantages. It's about finding a balance and identifying when each tool serves you best. The digital system is, of course, much more efficient, faster, more flexible, and can hold much more information than you're willing to write by hand. So, use that to your advantage. The analog system, however, is frictionless, meditative, and intentional, all things we need more of in our day to day lives.

THE TYPING RACE

Oh! Those bright and shiny digital tools! So addictive, with all their colors, customization, and categories... or am I the only one who enjoys all that? Digital tools, aside from being user friendly and efficient, have a great advantage in our hyper-connected world. It has never been more important to be able to share information, merge our planning tools, and collaborate with coworkers on a daily basis. This connectivity is impossible with an analog tool, which is why a digital platform is crucial for any tasks that require teamwork.

Digital tools also allow you to stay "connected." How many times have you left your house without your phone? I thought so... Chances are, whatever app you are using to hold your information has a version you can download to your phone or a cloud-based service, meaning your notes are with you everywhere you go. This instant accessibility has become essential in our rapidly-paced world.

Another massive advantage a digital platform has over analog, one that is kind of crucial for most of us, is the ability to remind you about pretty much anything. The automaticity means that you won't have to make the choice or even remember to follow through. Instead, you'll have a preprogrammed alert that will tell you what to do. This is a must.

Finally, probably my favorite digital asset is the search function. One click, a few keyboard strokes, and boom! You've got what you were looking for. I mean, it doesn't get more efficient than that. So, yes, the digital world has almost irreplaceable advantages, and yet, there is still great value in an analog system.

THE WRITING STROLL

I could write an entire essay romanticizing the feeling of writing on a blank page, but I gather most of you wouldn't enjoy that. So, let's just come to consensus that there is nothing quite like handwriting your thoughts. It's completely frictionless, there are no rules or boundaries, there is no limit to what you can do on paper; it's completely flexible and customizable. That's powerful, especially when it comes to capturing your ideas and letting your creativity flow. If you wanted to capture creativity with a digital tool, you'd probably be faced with labels you need to add, categories to assign, or a very limited format to explain your thoughts. More importantly, however, when you're capturing ideas or planning, an analog system protects your undivided attention. There're no notifications beeping, or a bunch of links, subcategories, lists, or apps that you can access with one click. Instead, planning on paper is a pensive practice that, combined with the lack of friction, can allow you to empty your brain and find clarity staring back at you. To me, it feels like your thoughts are no longer in your head; they're in your hand. Is that weird?

Even if that's not the case, we're so used to being hyper-connected to our thoughts, tasks, and external influences that we forget to look inward on a regular basis. Writing things down can provide you with the distance you need to observe and make clearheaded decisions about what's in front of you, whether that's tasks you want to get to, ideas you wish to pursue, or emotions you can't figure out. This is only possible because the process is slow and intentional, unlike on a digital platform.

Finally, handwriting is one of the best ways to extract important information. More often than not, typing is automatic, you type everything you hear, *verbatim*. Because handwriting isn't as "efficient," you're forced to pay attention and pull the bits and pieces that matter from the conversation. Again, the analog process inherently clarifies the idea. Plus, there's the whole creativity thing. Which you know is my favorite part of dot journaling.

The key to owning your journal planning is to find what works for you. Find how your favorite digital tools can support your journaling practice, or the other way around if you're mainly digital-based. I'm obsessed with apps, gadgets, technology and all things digital, which is why I use them as organizational tools in my productivity system. However, I can't live without my dot journal. And I would be a totally different person if I had to. It's provided me with so much clarity and focus that no app can even begin to emulate. So, let's find out how you can combine these tools to make your ideal planning system.

CALENDARS

Digital. Digital. Digital. One hundred percent. And, for one simple reason: notifications! Calendars are mainly used to note time-sensitive appointments, due dates, or events. Normally, we'll use our calendars to plan ahead. In any case, predicting the future is something we rarely excel at, which makes the "moving around tasks" function of a digital platform so convenient. Yes, you can scratch or white out in your dot journal, but when what you want is to move things around fast and without making a mess, a digital calendar is just a better option for this. However, what makes this a much better option for planning time sensitive appointments is the ability to notify you when necessary.

Aside from using the calendar to plan ahead, it can be used to *organize* the day. More specifically, to add a date and time to tasks. This allows to you batch similar tasks together and to calendar block your day in a way that makes the most sense to you and allows you to get all your tasks done.

BLOCKING AND BATCHING DIGITALLY

There are many ways to support your planning system with a digital calendar. For example, you might use your journal to brain dump everything that you need to get done—whether you're planning for the month, week, or day—and then plot that into your calendar in the most efficient way possible. You can use your journal to plan ahead and strategize on what needs to get done when, and then use your digital calendar to plot the due dates for these projects. You can also use your digital calendar to capture appointments on the go.

When planning for the week, for example, you could list everything that needs to get done in your journal, assign the day of the week you might want to get them done, and use your digital calendar to batch similar tasks together. Let's say you might need to record three different videos and take ten pictures of products for your website. You might list the specific tasks in your journal with any details and notes necessary and batch when you'll be doing each in your calendar. Maybe you decide to all take pictures on Tuesday from 2:00 to 4:00 p.m. If batching does not work with your existing commitments, you can find the best time to actually get those tasks done. For example, you might decide to film one video per day, each one right before going to work, after you've gotten dressed up for the day.

By assigning these tasks a date and specifically blocking that time to work on these things, you increase your chances of getting them done. Having a calendar allows you to see those empty spaces where you can dump tasks to be more efficient. Replicating a calendar like this in a journal is just a lot of work and not at all flexible.

You could do what Amy Landino does. In the evenings, use your journal to list the things that you want to get done the next day, and use the digital calendar to block in what order, when, and for how long you'll be working on each one of them.

MY PERFECT BALANCE

Or, you can do what I do. When I'm planning my month, I'll strategize, dump, write my goals, create trackers for those goals, and jot down things I want to get done in my journal. Then, I'll use my calendar to plot in the time-sensitive commitments, due dates and maybe map out when I want to be working on some things. Kind of like this:

MONTHLY CALENDAR

When it comes to planning the week or the day, I use my digital calendar to batch and calendar block when I'll be working on certain things. I don't transfer the specific tasks into my calendar; these stay in my journal. I'll simply block what kind of work I'll be doing, what project I'll be working on or what task batch I'd want to get done during that block of time. That looks something like this:

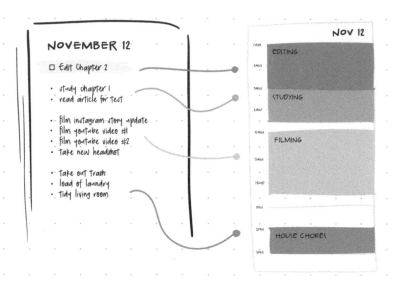

What matters is that you are able to see *when* it's better to get a specific task done and not just follow your to-do list without direction or prioritization. I use my journal as my thinking space. It's where all the little details live. My calendar, however, is where I get organized.

THE "WORK CALENDAR" ALTERNATIVE

Some people have very clear boundaries and totally different workflows for their work life and their personal life. They will, for example, do all their work planning on their digital calendars because of networking and efficiency, and use their journal for planning their personal lives. This is another way to make the best of both your digital and analog tools. If that's something that could work for you, I think it's a great idea because it'll provide you with the shutdown and boundaries you need to leave work at work and focus on yourself when you leave the office.

YOUR PERFECT BALANCE

When it comes to choosing between a digital or analog calendar, you might want to consider some key functional aspects. You need a system that works. Meaning, you make it to all your appointments because you know when they're happening, you meet your deadlines because you have a good enough preview of when they're due, and you organize your time according to what works best for you. Ideally, you want this system to hold everything in one place so you never double-book your time. More importantly, whatever system you use needs to be easy to *see* when you're getting things done and when you can efficiently group like things together so you can make the most out of your time.

I tried using my journal for a long time, but I didn't find it as efficient. I never referenced my Future Log. I was frustrated when I had to move an appointment and I didn't enjoy creating "calendar-like" spreads or "timetables." Plus, if you add nice colors, the digital calendar looks so pretty, and that's always motivating.

TASK MANAGERS

It's time to plan out your day. What do you do? Take out your computer, phone, or journal? If you've been using a digital task manager for ages, and your system works, who am I to tell you there's something better out there? By all means, do you. Find what works for you and stick to it. The consistency itself will grant you more results than the tools you choose to use. I will, of course, remind you to apply the principles to planning your day, but *where* you do it is up to you.

That being said, in my opinion, nothing compares to the essential role a daily to-do list fulfills. The Daily Log is where I answer, "What will I do today?" It allows me to really focus only on those tasks and forget about the other hundreds of to-do's I've gathered in other lists. It's the place where I think for that day. An analog system provides you with the pause necessary to consider if something is worth doing or not because of the simple fact that you have to write that task down, unlike digital task managers where your undone tasks automatically trail to the next day. By unconsciously forcing yourself to keep your to-do list to a minimum—since you don't want to write a page's worth of tasks—you're actively choosing what is worth your time and what's not. My digital calendar will help me rearrange those tasks, assign them a specific time, remind me of appointments, and give me an estimated schedule of my day, but the complete list of tasks, big and small—along with notes and signifiers— will be in my Daily Log. Regardless of what tool you use, what matters is that your system allows you to see at a glance what the important tasks for the day are and that you're taking action on those to-dos.

LISTS, LISTS, AND MORE LISTS

Don't get me wrong, I still use a digital task manager. What for? Themed lists. Basically, I use it to collect tasks that don't have to get done soon into their proper lists. Some examples are: At Home, On My Mac, To Call, X Project, Errands, To Buy, Sometime Soon, Someday, Movies to Watch, Books to Read, etc. The idea is to make it easier to tackle tasks by context. For example, if I'm picking up some stuff around the house and I have an hour to kill, I might open my "At Home" list and start getting those small tasks done. Or, if I'm running some errands, I can check my "Errands" list and see what else I can get done now that I'm already out of the house. It's important to note that these things are not time-sensitive and most certainly not move-the-needle kind of tasks. They're usually easy, little annoying things that just have to get done. I keep these in a digital task manager for convenience and because I have a lot of them so it's easier to drop them in an app's inbox and organize them later.

The other crucial way I leverage a digital task manager is to schedule recurring tasks. So, anything that needs to get done on a regular basis I'll add to a specific list in my to-do app and create the necessary notifications to make sure I get them done. Oh! And, of course, I use my digital task manager to pop in tasks/notes I need a reminder for, but we all do that already, right?

In the end, what matters is that your system makes it easy for you to know exactly what you're supposed to be doing at all times and where to find those tasks you've put on hold. Just because you want to handle all your tasks in a digital platform doesn't mean you can't use a journal anymore. Use whatever parts of the system work for you—use it to track, to write, to think, to capture, to detail ideas—do whatever you need to do on paper so you can be even more productive in your digital space.

DON'T BE AFRAID TO ACCESSORIZE

Find what parts of your system might need a digital accessory. Remember that it's not just about what can be done better in a digital platform, but rather what is not working on your current analog system that inevitably needs to be replaced or complimented with a digital tool. If it ain't broke, don't fix it, right?

NOTE TAKING

There are so many forms of note taking and so many different kinds of notes you might need to keep. My advice is to find what platform works best for each kind of note. For example, I use an app for academic note taking. Not just school notes, but also for things that I'm learning from sources like books, podcasts, lectures, courses, blog posts, etc. On the other hand, when it comes to brainstorming, jotting down ideas, and planning rough drafts, I'll use my journal. You might choose a different solution for notes on meetings than you will for notes on cooking recipes, and so on.

Try to think about what you will do with that note. If you'll need to share it, collaborate, search for it fairly quickly, or use parts of it to produce content, it might be best to do it digitally. If, on the other hand, you need to use those scribbles when planning, to grasp quick concepts to expand later, to gather rough ideas, or if you just wrote it to clear your head and won't be needing it at all, you might want to use an analog format. Because of the of the lack of friction and restrictions, it'll be easier to unleash your creativity.

Either way, I would advise you to pick a specific system for each of the kinds of notes you take and keep all of those in one place so that it's easy to find what you're looking for at any given time.

PROJECT PLANNING

The bottom line is project planning probably requires a level of detail a bit too complicated for an analog system. What ends up happening for me is that I'll brainstorm and create outlines and plans in my journal, but when it comes to in-depth planning, I'll refer to a digital tool that allows me to get organized, keep notes, add details and due dates, and collaborate with others. For example, right now I have all the details for this book, what stage each chapter is in, what illustrations need to be created, and the outlines and notes on all of it in my digital platform. On a day-to-day basis, I'll refer to that plan and incorporate the actions I need to take to my regular journaling practice, and I'll use my journal to brainstorm on what I'd like to include in each chapter.

Don't be afraid to combine your systems and create where it feels right at that moment. In the end, what you need is a place to hold most of the information so you can see at a glance what your progress is. This may vary from project to project.

HABIT TRACKING

This is one of the most famous uses of dot journaling and part of what makes this system so special. We'll go into detail in the next section. I think habit tracking in a digital vs. analog platform comes down to two things. One, preference. In what way do you get the most satisfaction of checking off a habit as done? Where are you more likely to get it done? Two, value. Habit tracking is worthless if you can't look back at your behavior and draw conclusions. The latter is why I believe that no digital tool quite compares to habit tracking in your journal. You're much more likely to analyze the data collected in your notebook than in an app, and this makes it more powerful. It allows you to see the progress for each of your habits with one glance. If you're using this on a regular basis, you'll notice how you adjust your behavior as you go and not just at the end of the tracking period.

You can always support your tracking practice by having an app to list all the habits you need to get done that day. Do whatever works for you. When it comes to tracking, what matters is what you do with the information. You just have to find the tool that allows you to do the most. And, more importantly, use one that prompts you to actually stick to your habits.

QUICK CAPTURE

In the previous chapters, we talked about the importance of capturing your thoughts, ideas, and appointments immediately. Well, sometimes you don't have your journal at hand. Pulling out your notebook and finding a pen in the black hole that is your purse takes just long enough for you to forget that brilliant thought. I get it. This is why I rely on a digital quick capture system in these kinds of situations...because guess what is always at hand? My phone.

It's important that you find a way to complement your dot journaling practice with a quick capture function that is available to you at all times. This will help you tuck away those open loops and focus on whatever you're doing at the moment. If your dot journal isn't doing the job, you can use your digital quick capture tool as your Task Inbox. If this is something you rely on heavily, then you can designate a day and frequency with which you will go through this inbox. I go through mine once a week. I suggest you start with a system that allows you to capture all kinds of thoughts (notes, ideas, tasks) so that you have only one inbox to go through.

E-JOURNALING

A digital dot journal is basically a PDF file with space to create spreads and hyperlinks to make it easier to navigate within the document. There are lots of advantages and disadvantages to this practice, but I think the significance of those really depend on each person. For example, because I'm such a perfectionist, when I'm using a digital dot journal, I will move things around, change colors, edit, erase, and rewrite things a million times, whereas with paper, I feel a bit less compelled to create a perfect spread. Others might actually experience the opposite. In the end, a digital dot journal can be used pretty much like any journal with the exception of turning off the digital space when planning. In my opinion, if the pros outweigh the cons and it works for you, by all means, go digital! More than the platform, what matters is what you're doing with these tools and how you are planning. Digital dot journals are just not my cup of tea.

FROM SKETCH TO REALITY

My journal is where I brain dump every little thing that comes to mind. It's where I sketch out my life, where I write my dreams, and where I can plan and reflect on pretty much anything. I find the clarity that I need by emptying my mind. I jot down everything, and then I take those tasks or ideas and expand on them in my digital platforms where I'll organize the information, link it, share it, collaborate, categorize and really develop those projects to the very last detail. Through this process, I'm able to turn those sketches that have been so carefully captured and transform them into a reality.

I now look at my journal as a snippet of what my life looked like during the months I used that notebook. I love using it to keep track of *everything*, to dive deep into my personal life, my thoughts, my growth process, and to freely plan ahead without any friction or constraints. I go crazy creating Collections to capture parts of my life. I balance this freedom and creative expression with a rigid digital system that allows me to organize my to-do's, projects, ideas, content, knowledge, information, and pretty much everything else.

Feel free to take my advice with a grain of salt. Find what works for you. My official recommendation is to try to find a system that will give you consistency. This might mean doing all of your planning in your journal and supporting that with digital tools to set up reminders, store your notes, and expand on projects. Or, you might be like me, supporting my analog dumping practice with a calendar that I'll update in each planning session based on the information in my notebook. What you need is a system that safely stores your information, so your brain trusts it, and that is organized, so you'll know exactly what you need to be doing next.

My greatest rule of thumb for finding this perfect balance is that you should know where everything is. At any given time, if you want to access something, you should know exactly where to find it. If you don't, it most likely means your system is too complicated.

PART III

Journal Your Goals for Life

CHAPTER 8

A Goal without a Plan

Do you know the ending of that quote? "A goal without a plan is just a wish," by the one and only Antoine de Saint-Exupéry.

My friends sometimes ask me why they even need to set up goals, and my answer is always the same. If you want to float through life, doing only what the world tells you to do, living only as far as the next week of your life, you don't *need* goals. I won't judge you. There is nothing wrong with you. You can keep living life as it happens to you. But, if you want to get somewhere, if there is anything you desperately want out of life, if there is anything you're willing to chase, then you need to take that thing, put it on paper, call it a goal, and get it done.

Unfortunately, a goal is not enough. This is the part where I try to sweet talk them into letting me help them make a plan, because a goal without a plan is just a wish. You can keep making wishes or refusing to define your goals just make sure you're ready to realize, a year from now, that you're practically the same person you were a year ago and that you've accomplished just about enough to stumble through the year. Be ready to realize that life *happened to you*, you didn't make anything happen. Instead—since I started setting goals—this is what I realize at the end of the year: "When did I get all of these things done? How did I accomplish so much? I don't even remember when I made the time for it. I don't remember struggling to achieve this. *¿En qué momento hice todo esto?* (In what moment did I get all of this done?)" I'm not saying I'm perfect and that I achieve all of my goals all of the time. Of course, I don't. I still have things that cripple me and that seem too hard, things that go unfinished, but I always get *something* done. At least one thing. I'm not saying it's easy. I'm saying it's worth it. Because, who doesn't want to look back on the month, the year, the past five years, their life and be proud of what they've accomplished? Who doesn't want to say they *did* it?

If you don't want that, if you genuinely aren't interested, that's alright. You can skip to the next section because this probably isn't for you. But if you do want it, and maybe you're a little scared, or you don't know where to start, or you're not sure exactly what it is that you want, but you know you want something, keep reading. I'm going to make this simple for you, because all you need to get started is a plan.

MY MAGICAL METHOD

Just like with everything else, all you have to do to succeed is take it one step at a time. After hundreds of "Monthly Review" sessions (sitting at the end of the month to review my progress on my goals and my life in general), many failed attempts at achieving them, along with, of course, some successful attempts, I finally realized what the planning essentials are that will highly increase my chances of achieving a goal. That four-part method is what I'll be sharing with you in this chapter.

If at this very moment, all you can think about is how daunting and overwhelming planning your goals seems and how long and tiresome this sounds, don't worry, you're not alone. That's normal, and you should be scared. Because: What if this changes your life? What if you can't unknow this? How easy is it going to be for you to achieve goals then? Don't be scared of how complicated it can be because I'll be here to guide you through every step of the way. Hopefully, by the end of this chapter, you'll realize it's so much more attainable than it seems. Just look at it this way: Goal: Figure out how to plan for my goals. Plan: Let Andrea do all the work. Action: Keep reading.

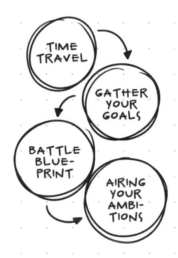

Time Travel: Find your dreams. Dig deep and figure what it is that you want, and why.

Gathering Your Goals: Define the actual goals, the words you will write down on paper to keep you motivated.

Battle Blueprint: Identify how this fits into your life. Build the path to your goals by breaking them down into bite size pieces and actionable steps.

Airing Your Ambitions: Put goals out into the world and revisit them on a regular basis.

In summary, first we figure out what it is that we actually want, then we turn that into a goal, we create a plan on how it is we can achieve this goal, and finally, as we are executing this plan, we revise our progress and make the necessary adjustments to ensure we'll be successful. I told you, it's pretty simple. Let's do this.

TIME TRAVEL

"The key to realizing a dream is to focus not on success but significance—and then even the small steps and little victories along your path will take on greater meaning."

—*Oprah Winfrey*

FIND YOUR DREAMS. DIG DEEP AND FIGURE WHAT IT IS THAT YOU WANT, AND WHY.

Why? Why do you want to drink more water, save more money, work out every day, build a brand, get your master's degree, spend more time with your family, drink less alcohol, read more books or whatever is this that is going through your head right now? Why? There must be a reason. I'm not saying it has to be this huge life-changing purpose. It can be something as small as "because I really feel like it right now," but there is always a reason. The clearer that vision is, the likelier it is you'll achieve your goals. Chasing something, anything, immediately creates a path in an otherwise crowded cluster of options. Take Maze A, for example; there is an exit somewhere, I promise...but, where do you start? Where do you turn? Where are you going? Now, take Maze B. Do you see the path? Can you solve it? Which maze is easier to "walk" through?

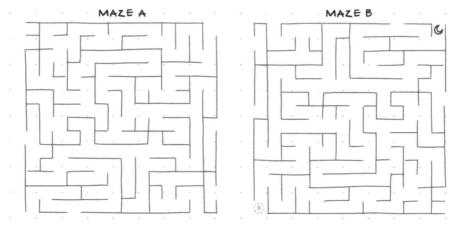

Want to hear a secret? It's the same maze, the same exact maze, rotated and flipped. The marks of Maze B give you direction, and more importantly, they give you a reason to keep going. Why would you even solve a maze that has no exit marked? For all you know, it doesn't even have a solution... This is what happens when you become clear about what your why is. You find your exit mark.

How do you find your why? Yeah, I thought you'd ask. This is where "Time Travel" comes in. The idea is to picture yourself in the future, in the past, out of the present, and to get as much information as you can. Find who you want to be and how you want your life to look.

VISUALIZATION

Let's start with the future. I normally do this once or twice a year when I want to determine my long-term goals. I write this in the first pages of my journal. Picture yourself a year from now, five years from now, however long you want and really think about who you'd like to be. Think about how you want to feel, what you have accomplished, and how you feel about that. What does your environment look like? What do you envision for your life? What is making you happy and proud in that moment? How far have you come? What kind of person do you want to be? Again, how do you feel? The feelings part sounds cheesy, but trust me, it is so important because in the end, you can have achieved a million things during the year without any of them actually bringing you any happiness or pride.

So, visualize how you want to *feel* at the end of the year. Journal it, record it on a voice note, draw it out, talk about it with that someone you trust—do whatever it is you have to do to put it out into the real world. Don't be afraid to dream big; this is not the moment to hold yourself back or be realistic (that's coming in a few pages). Most importantly, be completely honest with yourself. I know, it takes practice, but the more you visualize your future, the more real and achievable it becomes. And, of course, write it down. This is so important. Open your journal and dump all your thoughts into the page so they become tangible and no longer an abstract compound of ideas floating in the back of your head. The simple act of writing down one-page's worth of the person you wish to be someday will have a tremendous influence on the person you are now. You don't want to forget that thing that's going to keep you moving once you're actually pursuing these goals.

If you need a little guidance, you can maybe start to look at what your future looks like for each of the categories in your life. Mel Robbins, one of my favorite motivational and keynote speakers, uses these categories to define her goals: Body, Work/School, Money, Love Life, Friendships, Self-Worth.*

> *It's okay not to want to work on an area of your life, or to be satisfied with it. The time will come when you do want to work on it. Be honest with yourself.

This future version of yourself that you are aspiring to become is your "why." Everything you do, all the small goals you achieve are *because* you want to become that person. That vision you are chasing is your why. From this uncensored picture of your life, you'll start to notice the patterns and the things you really want to accomplish. You'll start to see what your possible *goals* are. You'll start to see opportunity and a clearer path of how to go about your "year." There is no denying what it is you really want, and now there is no reason to not go after it. Your future self has all the answers; you just have to ask. Once you find your why, we can start to define the goals you might want to set to get there.

WHAT'S MY VISION?

THINGS I'M GRATEFUL FOR:

THINGS THAT ENERGIZE ME:

THINGS THAT DRAIN ME:

THINGS I WANT TO DO MORE OF:

For the following prompts, picture your future self.

HOW DO I WANT TO FEEL THROUGHOUT THE YEAR?

What does my environment look like? What do I envision for my life? What is making me happy and proud? How far have I come? What kind of person do I want to be?

WHAT DO I WANT TO HAVE ACCOMPLISHED?

PROGRESS REVIEW

Like I said, I only do this maybe once or twice a year, and it gives me the big picture of how I want the rest of my year to go. Time traveling into the past, however, *that* I do constantly. Well, once a month, to be exact. This is part of my "Monthly Review," where I go through my journal, look at all of the things I've tracked and done over the past month, and review my progress.

The past is the other place your new goals come from. What worked? What didn't work? What do you want more of? What drove you in the past? The way I figure these questions out is by constantly revising my progress and my life. This is key to actually accomplishing your goals because it kickstarts your motivation on a more regular basis. By constantly looking back, you'll know what you no longer want and what you have been craving for the future. More details on this are coming, I promise.

GATHERING YOUR GOALS

gather your goals

DEFINE THE ACTUAL GOALS, THE WORDS YOU WILL WRITE DOWN ON PAPER TO KEEP YOU MOTIVATED.

Oh! The mess we just created...I know. All of your goals and ideas are flying around everywhere (hopefully, in the pages of your journal), and you have so much you want to do, but where do we begin? It's time to shape those ideas into beautifully designed goals. Now, let's flip the page on our journal and start gathering all the ideas/

dreams/aspirations you came up with during your time travels. Jot down a few sentences of what your possible goals for the year could be. Try to minimize this list to the goals that inspire you the most and that would have the greatest impact on your life. If this is your first time planning for goals, I'd say stick to no more than five goals for now. Honestly, you can even start with just one. When this becomes second nature you can choose as many goals as you see fit.

Once you have your list of "goals" in your journal, the next step is to categorize them into what kind of goal they are. (A bit tedious, I know, but bear with me. This is important.) There are three kinds of goals that we tend to create, I call them: Someday, Current, and Ladder Goals. Categorizing your goals into these buckets is going to give you some clarity as to what "actions/ tasks" you need to plan in order to achieve these goals.

1. SOMEDAY GOALS

These are the things that you can do in one day and that don't really need much planning or effort. There are probably not many steps to get these done other than just going and doing them... *someday* this year. For example, I want to visit X place in my city this year.

2. CURRENT GOALS

By current, I don't necessarily mean **"in the present**," but more like the **"flow of water."** Our daily habits and our patterns create a current in our life: a flow, moving continuously in a certain direction. They create a lifestyle; they create who we become. The good news is you can take control of the current in your life. You are not powerless. You do not *have* to drift with the current because, unlike a body of water, you can control the direction of the stream.

ADV — BELONGING TO THE PRESENT TIME.

NOUN — A BODY OF WATER OR AIR MOVING IN A DEFINITE DIRECTION.

Current goals are the ones you create to change the direction of your life, whether you plan them out in detail or just keep them in the back of your mind, working toward them unconsciously. They are the goals you make when you want to do more or less of something. These are things like drink more water, read more, pray more, drink less alcohol, eat less junk food, go to sleep earlier, etc. These are usually things that you want to attract to your life in the present moment. For whatever reason, a current goal is something you want more of in your life. Hopefully, one day, they might become a permanent part of who you are. Not a habit goal, for example, but more of a ladder or a life goal. By actually doing more or less of these things, you are shaping the current, your patterns, your habits, and most importantly, your future.

3. LADDER GOALS

These are the goals that are really more like projects. They are usually long term and have multiple subtasks you need to get done in order to achieve them. For example: "I want to run a marathon this year." You're going to have to train for it, decide how much you'll be running to start with, how much you need to increase this to reach your goal in time, when you will be training, and adjust accordingly as you progress. There are steps to follow, and just like a ladder, the only way to get to the top is by climbing one step at a time. This is completely different than "I want to run more," which is a Current Goal. For that goal, you can simply decide to go on a run a certain number of days a week or go running in the park every Sunday. Do you see the difference? Other examples of Ladder Goals might be to open a business, start a YouTube channel, get a second job, finish college early, get your master's degree, move to another apartment, create a website, train for a competition in your favorite sport, travel during your two-week vacation, etc. All of these things need a long-term plan and milestones to help you actually achieve those goals by their due date.

Let's start with a tangible example. Let me introduce you to Samantha, a lovely woman who's goals I've just made up. She'll help us out with our examples. We'll take Sam's rough draft of her 2021 goals and assign them to categories.

Sam's Goals

—— CATEGORIZED ——

WORK OUT REGULARY	◉	CURRENT
DRINK MORE WATER	◉	CURRENT
VISIT DISNEY WORLD	★	SOMEDAY
MANAGE MY MONEY	◉	CURRENT
START A BLOG	◆	LADDER
READ MORE BOOKS	◉	CURRENT

S PECIFIC
M EASURABLE
A CTIONABLE
R ELEVANT
T IME-BOUND
E VALUATED
R EVIEWED

REFINING OUR GOALS

The intention is there and we now have a rough draft of what our possible goals are, but they need just a little more polishing. The phrasing matters. It changes the actions you'll take, it changes the tone and intention, and most importantly, if you're going to be constantly looking at your goals, don't you want them to be pleasing to read? Mastering the art of writing your goals in a way that motivates you to go after them gives you clear direction. It also inspires you to keep going and will make it so much easier for you to actually achieve those goals. It will give you confidence to believe that you can do what you said you were going to do. This mastery, however, comes with time and practice. In the meantime, the acronym "SMARTER" can be your cheat sheet for rewriting your goals in a more inspiring fashion, one that actually leads to seeing those goals accomplished.

In my opinion, however, there are other things that are crucial when it comes to gathering your goals.

A GOOD WHY

If there is no reason behind your goal, are you really going to be motivated to accomplish it? Sometimes the why can be as simple as "because I need this in my life" or something much bigger like "because it's the first step to my dream life." It doesn't matter what your why is, it only matters that you have one and that this goal is something you genuinely want. Hopefully, this why became clear when you were time traveling.

IN YOUR CONTROL

A goal like "get 1,000 new followers on Instagram" is not necessarily in your control. You can do everything right, put in the work, and still not get those followers because it is not your choice—other people decide if they follow you or not. Similarly, a goal like "getting a job promotion" is not in your control. Even if you are the best person for the job, you could still not be chosen—it does not depend on you. I'm not saying that wanting those things is bad. It's great that you want them, but they should not be your goal. Instead, you should set a goal that focuses on the process to get to that "number of followers" or "job promotion." Perhaps reword your goals into something like this: "I want to post one piece of Instagram content every day this month" or "I want to create one new project for my company." Focus your energy into the *work* that might get you to the top. By doing this, you become in control of reaching your goal, and thus, you are way more likely to be successful.

ACHIEVABLE

Dreaming is great, I'm all for it... but when it comes to choosing your goals, you gotta be realistic. You're not going to get your four-year college degree in one year, you simply can't. More importantly, look at your schedule. How much time do you really have to dedicate to your goals? If you're already working a 9-to-5 job and have four children and a house to take care of, odds are you won't have the time or energy to build a business, start a blog, train for a marathon, and travel all in one year. Maybe you only have time to do *one* of those things this year. That's fine; be realistic. I'm not saying you should drop your expectations or not shoot for anything. Just be aware of how much time you actually have to work on these goals within your existing lifestyle.

POSITIVE CONNOTATION

Ideally, your goals should be positive. You don't want them to constantly remind you of a fault you have. Try as much as you can to avoid using negatives in your goal statement. Try to focus on the good and the things that you should do rather than the things you should not. For example: "I want to change my negative self-talk" could be reworded as "I want to practice more positive self-talk."

Let's take Samantha's Goals, for example, and reword them to make them more achievable.

Sam's Goals

REFINED

★ VISIT DISNEY WORLD → VISIT DISNEY WORLD ON MY BIRTHDAY

◉ WORK OUT REGULARY → WORK OUT EVERY WEEKDAY

◉ DRINK MORE WATER → DRINK 2L WATER PER DAY

◉ MANAGE MY MONEY → CREATE A BUDGET & TRACK SPENDINGS

◉ READ MORE BOOKS → READ 6 BOOKS (2 SELF DEVELOPMENT)

◆ START A BLOG → BLOG READY BY JUNE

MY GOALS

DRAFT

Write down a potential goal statement. You can use categories in your life as a guide: Body, Work/School, Relationships, Money, etc...

REFINED

Turn that into an achievable goal statement by using the SMARTER acronym and remembering that a goal needs to be achievable, in your control, and with a positive connotation.

NOW WHAT?

You have a list of goals, you know what kind of goal each one is, you've reworded them into inspiring statement, and you've created a Collection in your journal that holds them, but the rest of the page is still blank. What do we do next to actually achieve those goals? Well, that depends on what kind of goals they are.

BATTLE BLUEPRINT

IDENTIFY HOW THIS FITS INTO YOUR LIFE. BUILD THE PATH TO YOUR GOALS BY BREAKING THEM DOWN INTO BITE SIZED PIECES AND ACTIONABLE STEPS.

The biggest reason why people quit is because they are looking at the whole picture and not the simple next step. When you look at the entirety of a project, you can instantly become overwhelmed by hundreds of steps you have yet to take, but if you focus on the best next step, there's no excuse to stay still. If at this very moment I was thinking about how I yet have eleven chapters to plan, write, draw, revise, edit, re-read, and re-write, I would be going crazy (I'm kind of going crazy now, but okay...). I would probably not have sat down to work on the book in the first place because "Where do I even start?" Instead, all I had to do today was sit down for twenty-five minutes to edit this chapter. That's it. So simple, so easy to actually pull off. People get overwhelmed when they fail to break their goals down into digestible, actionable steps and when they fail to focus on that simple task instead of the whole picture. The good news is that you can beat this resistance by creating a Battle Blueprint, essentially a breakdown of how you'll make these goals happen. How will you win?

You can visualize all you want, but without action, nothing will ever get done. So, for every single goal you create, we need an action you can take in order to get one step closer to the finish line. We'll outline these in our Blueprint. The actions you need to take, though, depend on what kind of goal it is. This is where the categorization of our goals comes in. If your goal is a **Someday** one, all you need to do is decide what day of the year you'll be doing this and book it or add it to your calendar. If your goal is a **Current** one, then create a habit, ritual, or rule that will help you stay consistent with your goal. For example, if my goal is to read more, I could create a habit of reading fifteen minutes a day before bed; if my goal is to eat less junk food, I could create the rule that I will eat junk food only during the weekends. If your goal is a **Ladder Goal**, then you will need to create a long term plan, a time line with due dates and potential milestones that I like to call a Milestone Map. This flowchart will take you from categorizing your goals to identifying the kind of action steps you might need to take.

So, let's break Sam's goals down into tangible, measurable actions that she can do regularly. Notice how Current goals have habits and routines as actions while Someday goals have a date, and Ladder goals have a Milestone Map reference.

Battle Blueprint

GOALS

ACTIONS

SOMEDAY

GOALS	ACTIONS
VISIT DISNEY WORLD	CALENDAR FEBRARY 23-27
WORK OUT EVERY DAY	M/W: UPPER BODY T/T: LOWER BODY F: YOGA
DRINK 2L OF WATER PER DAY	FILL MY 1L WATER BOTTLE TWICE A DAY
BUDGET & TRACK EXPENSES	MONTHLY BUDGET & MONTHLY REVIEW
READ 6 BOOKS (2 SELF DEV.)	READ 15 MINUTES DAILY
LAUNCH BLOG BY JUNE	(MILESTONE MAP) WORK MINIMUM 4 HOURS PER WEEK

CURRENT

LADDER

Samantha lives in Miami, and one of her goals this year is to go to Disney World, since she hasn't visited it yet. There is little planning that goes into this, since Disney is just a few hours away from Miami—all she has to do is buy the tickets and go! This is why this is a Someday Goal. All she has to do is set the date in her calendar and wait until that day comes.

For Current Goals, it's important to define what are you going to do on a regular basis to achieve the objective. This is the gold mine. If there is anything you take from this chapter on goals, let it be this: you achieve your goals on a daily basis. Every time you dedicate the time to work on them, you are one step closer. When are you going to make the time? Be as specific as possible: What? When? How? We'll talk more about this in the following chapters.

Finally, for our Ladder Goals, we need to create a list of milestones and do some reverse engineering. As you work on your project, you'll realize that there are probably more things you had to do that you didn't even know about, and that some of your milestone due dates might have to change, and that's okay. The idea is to create a flexible map of what you should be doing by when so you can take it one step at a time. Transform this huge goal into digestible bite-sized pieces that you can actually incorporate into your routine. If Sam's Ladder Goal is to create a blog, her milestone map might look something like this:

GOAL: LAUNCH A BLOG ON JUNE 1ST

JANUARY: BRANDING & RESEARCH

Week 1: Brand indentity
Week 2: Create logo + Brand aesthetic
Week 3: Research tools (website, apps, photos)
Week 4: Research skills (marketing, writing)

Routine: Work for 1-2 hrs on weeknights, after work.

FEBRUARY: BUILD THE WEBSITE

Routine: Work for 1-2 hrs on weeknights, after work.

MARCH: BRAINSTORM & PLAN

Week 8: Research similar blogs.
Week 9: Come up with 10 ideas for potential blog posts + outlines
Week 10 & 11: Experiment and find the best time to write within my schedule and writing goal per week.

Routine: Work at night, after dinner.

APRIL: WRITE MINIMUM 5 BLOG POSTS

MAY: LAST DETAILS FOR LAUNCH

NOTES:

Don't worry, I'll show you how to get there in the next chapter. Great! Now, you have a vision of your future, clear inspiring goals, and an action plan, but how do you keep up with this as the months go by?

BATTLE BLUEPRINT

GOALS
What do you wish to accomplish?

ACTIONS
What can you do to make that happen?

AIRING YOUR AMBITIONS

PUT IT OUT INTO THE WORLD AND REVISIT THIS ON A REGULAR BASIS.

You know that really cool t-shirt that is crumbled in some dark corner of your closet, that you didn't even remember you had, but when you happen to clean your closet (once every never) you're so thrilled you found it because you love it so much and you can't wait to wear it again all the time (after it's properly disinfected, of course)? Don't let your goals be that t-shirt...

What I mean is: are your goals crumbled into some dark corner of a notebook you never open? How are you going to remember what they are? How are they going to inspire you every day? Your goals should be somewhere you can see them, out in the world. On your desktop, magnetized to your fridge, on a Post-it on your bathroom mirror, behind your door, as a screensaver on your phone... in your journal with a bookmark on it. Anywhere! As long as you see them!

Having a plan is essential, but the execution is more important. The whole point of making a plan at all is to make that execution as easy as possible, but you still have to put in the work. The key to actually achieving your goals is understanding that nothing is going to change or happen if you don't make the time for it. If you don't take those ten minutes you wanted to spend reading every day, if you don't create an "appointment" with yourself to make progress on your goal, how do you expect to see the result? Put it on your calendar! The initial drive that comes with an idea and that new-found motivation of turning it into a goal, unfortunately, fades if you let it. Don't let it. Make sure you are looking at your goals on a regular basis, so they motivate you to take action. By "Airing," I literally mean put your goals into the atmosphere, right where you can't ignore them.

VERB PUT INTO THE ATMOSPHERE, FRESHEN.

Okay, so how overwhelmed are you on a scale of one to ten? I know, we've covered *a lot*, and I'm sure it seems complicated, but I'm going to show you how simple applying these principles can be. Before we get into that, though, we still need to discuss one of the most crucial skills when it comes to achieving some goals and working through a project: Long-Term Planning.

CHAPTER 9

The Milestone Map and Long Term Planning

Just to give you a quick recap: When we're defining the actions we need to take for each of our goals, it's helpful to think about *what kind* of goal it is. Once you figure that out, planning entails setting up a due date and deciding how you'll make your way there. I call this a Milestone Map. This map is essentially a timeline that will walk you through the tiny steps you need to take in order to achieve that goal.

We'll cover the basic principles first. Throughout this chapter, I'll demonstrate what this would look like with Samantha's "Launch a Blog" Ladder Goal. Just like with the rest of the chapters, breaking down this process might make it seem lengthy, but in reality, if you understand the idea behind each of the steps, you'll be able go through it fairly quickly.

REVERSE ENGINEERING

When I was younger, mornings weren't such a blissful time for me as they are today. I was either sharing the bathroom with two sisters or rushing my dad and my brother so we wouldn't be late for school. I always hated being late. I remember the embarrassment that overpowered me when I had to do the walk of shame into an already focused classroom. I remember that I would pace outside the classroom for five minutes before I had the gathered the courage to walk in late. Quite counterproductive, but hey, I was ten! For the record, I still hate being late, but at a pretty young age, I learned how to avoid it. That's not even the most important part. I learned something that my friends wouldn't learn until a decade later.

On a random, beachside evening conversation with my dad, I mentioned that I didn't know at what time I should wake up the following morning. Very patiently, he explained:

"Well, that's easy. At what time do you have to be in school?"

"7:45"

"Alright, and it's a thirty-five-minute drive. So, subtract that. We're at 7:10." he said.

"What else do you need to do?"

"Shower."

"How long will that take?" he asked.

"Ten minutes."

"Alright, subtract ten minutes. We're at 7:00. What else?"

"Get dressed and get ready. That's like twenty minutes. So 6:40." I quickly replied.

"Alright, keep going."

"Eat breakfast and brush my teeth. Another twenty minutes. So, 6:20. Pack my bags, five minutes. 6:15."

"Anything else?"

"Nope."

"So, at what time do you have to wake up?"

"6:15!" I concluded. The idea was so simple. How could I have never thought of this?

At a really young age, I learned what we call in the productivity world "Reverse Engineering." The basic principle: start with the due date, estimate the amount of time each milestone will take, and work your way back until you find the starting point.

However, you can't always choose the starting point. Sometimes, you're given a certain amount of time to complete a project. The concept still applies. First, figure out what the milestones are. For example:

- **Goal:** read a ten-chapter book.

- **Time frame:** due in five weeks.

- **Milestones:** each chapter (ten milestones).

- **Goal plan:** align the milestones with the total time you have.

- **Reverse engineering:** read two chapters per week to finish the book in five weeks.

See? Simple. Alright, maybe that's an oversimplification of it, but you get the point.

I kind of have to mention that we never made it to school on time...BUT! It wasn't because reverse engineering doesn't work, but because he neglected one of the most crucial steps in reverse engineering: Add some wiggle room! Humans have a tendency to imagine our future selves as superheroes. We overestimate our performance, underestimate the amount of time it might take to do something, and always picture the best-case scenario. But life happens and most likely, it's not exactly as you planned. We're not robots and sticking to very confined schedules is not in our nature. So, do your future self a favor and add some wiggle room. Just, as a habit, always assume that something will disrupt your plans and it's better to be prepared.

This skill is what has made it possible for me to work on multiple projects at a time, to avoid procrastination, and to execute them while still enjoying the process. You can't always put your best work forward if you're rushing to meet a deadline. Of course, life happens, and that may end up being the case anyway, but for the most part, being able to complete what you envisioned in a timely fashion is a rare skill, one that will set you apart from the crowd.

Of course, the projects you might have in mind are probably much more complicated than getting ready for school. So, let me show you how to plan for long-term goals.

STEP 1: START AT THE END

Before we can make our next move, we have to decide where we're going. What is your goal? What will the end result of this project look like? Hopefully, this all became clear when you were actually defining your goals. You should now have a clear why and a clear result. And, of course, the due date for this project. Anyway, we did all this stuff already in the previous chapter, right? Without a precise north star to follow, you'll find yourself lost more often than necessary. Start with the ending.

STEP 2: BREAK IT DOWN

Just like I needed to know all the things I needed to do in the morning in order to get to school on time, you need to figure out what most of the things you need to get done for your project are. My solution: braindump. At this point, there is no order in your head and the tasks will just pop in without structure. That's fine. Don't worry about organizing anything right now, just dump all your thoughts into your journal. Let your mind flow.

Goal: Launch a Blog By June

BRAINDUMP

- pick a theme
- blog name
- research a website builder
- create website
- write 5 blogs before launch
- pick branding colors
- research pinterest for marketing
- create a pinterest account
- reasearch a place for stock photos
- create a schedule for content creation
- pinterest template for each blog post
- plan a month's worth of content
- research about ads on blog posts

When you have a pretty good idea of what your potential tasks are, you can start grouping them or categorizing them to create milestones. These are, essentially, mini-goals that add up to your big goal. There is no one-size-fits-all guide to finding the milestones for every project. However, I find it useful to put it all in front of me (in my braindump) and then start organizing it in the way that makes the most sense to me. Of course, there are many right ways to go about a project. Find the one that works for you. Follow your own logic, because you are the one who's gonna stick to that plan. How does it make sense for you to work? What can you group together? What can you batch? What categories are obvious? Is there a specific order in which things need to get done? You don't have to ask all of these questions, but they might help you figure out what the actual milestones are. Most projects work in phases, each one building up on the last. Remember that the objective is to break the huge overwhelming goal into attainable, actionable steps. The more you do this, the easier it'll be. So, for launching a blog, these are the mini-goals that make sense to me:

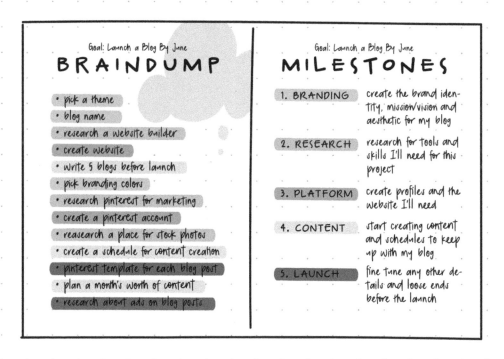

Goal: Launch a Blog By June

BRAINDUMP

- pick a theme
- blog name
- research a website builder
- create website
- write 5 blogs before launch
- pick branding colors
- research pinterest for marketing
- create a pinterest account
- reasearch a place for stock photos
- create a schedule for content creation
- pinterest template for each blog post
- plan a month's worth of content
- research about ads on blog posts

Goal: Launch a Blog By June

MILESTONES

1. BRANDING — create the brand iden-tity, mission/vision and aesthetic for my blog

2. RESEARCH — research for tools and skills I'll need for this project

3. PLATFORM — create profiles and the website I'll need

4. CONTENT — start creating content and schedules to keep up with my blog

5. LAUNCH — fine tune any other de-tails and loose ends before the launch

Goal:

BRAINDUMP

List everything you can think of that you might need to do for your Ladder Goal

. . . .

Goal:

MILESTONES

Group those to-dos into categories and form potential milestones.

STEP 3: ATTACH IT TO A TIMELINE

In this step, we'll give our project a time frame. Try not to over-complicate it for yourself. Go back to the basics of reverse engineering. Figure out either when you need to start, or how long you should spend working on each milestone.

The idea here is to try to link your milestones to a timeline. This is important not only because it creates urgency, but because it defines a clear start and finish line for each milestone. Referring back to the example I gave earlier about reading a ten-chapter book in five weeks: For the following week, you only have to read chapters one and two. This automatically reduces the overwhelm you were feeling when you were thinking about reading the entire book. Limiting a certain time frame to one mini-goal creates a tunnel vision that leaves all distractions and anxieties in the dark. All you have to focus on is the next milestone. That's it, no big picture. No staggering number of tasks to get done.

Taking apart your goal also allows you to stay passionate about it. This is because normally, at the beginning of a project, your motivation is off the charts, but over time, as you're faced with cumbersome work, motivation fades. By breaking your goals down, each milestone comes with its own dose of motivation. What I mean is, every time you complete a milestone you boost your motivation, and that will push you through the next milestone. This creates the satisfaction of accomplishing something, it creates results within a larger project, and in turn, inspires you to keep going. I should know, I celebrate every time I finish writing a chapter. This just makes me feel like I'm moving forward, and that's the greatest catalyst of all.

At the start of outlining your project, when it's time to think about the big picture and create a long term plan, keep it as simple as possible. Allow the milestones to be mini-projects.

They might even have multiple steps within each one, that's fine. Keep it simple. I like to think of this initial time line as a compass that shows me if I'm on track as I work on my goal. For example, if on my timeline I stipulated that I was going to read two chapters per week, and it's the end of the first week and I've only read half a chapter, something needs to change in order for me to meet my deadline. At the beginning of our Launch a Blog project, I would limit my timeline to something like this:

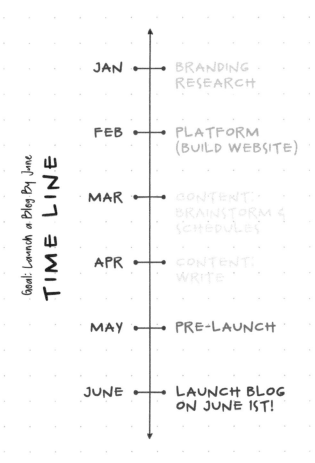

You can add as much detail as you want. However, this is my advice: Try to remember that life is going to happen, and your plans might have to change anyway. This is not supposed to be a strict one-exit-only kind of path. Instead, look at this outline as your guide to rely on through this rocky road. All you need is a general idea of the pace you need to be working at and what the due dates for the milestones you designed are.

Goal:

TIME LINE

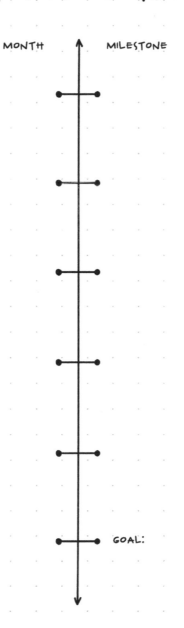

MONTH   MILESTONE

GOAL:

STEP 4: BUILD THE MILESTONE MAP

Great! So far, you've set a clear goal, you've broken down that goal into milestones, and you've framed them in a timeline. However, all your plans are hypotheticals until you give them a date and time in your calendar. This is where the Milestone Map comes in. The spread delineates when you'll be doing what. Meaning, in these few pages, you'll be plotting during what weeks or months you'll be working on each part of your project. Since we can't read into the future, we won't plan every single detail yet. However, whatever we do plan for gives us enough instruction to know what our next move should be. These few pages in your journal will become the blueprint for your project.

THE TRAIN OF THOUGHT

Alright, let's get started. The point of the Milestone Map is to help us dissect our project or goal into actionable steps. You want to boil it down to the very next thing you have to do in order to move forward with your project. You already started breaking your goal down when you created its milestones. Now, we want to take it a step further and break those milestones down into tasks. How do we do this? Well, I follow a simple train of thought:

GOAL

MONTHLY MILESTONE(S)

WEEKLY OUTCOME(S)

ROUTINE TO ACHIEVE THIS

LADDER OF THOUGHT

- What is my goal?

- What milestone(s) am I working on this month?

- What outcome(s) can I produce this week that will get me closer to that milestone?

- What *routine* will I implement to ensure I have the time to produce that outcome?

In other words, what are the actions that I will take on a regular basis to make sure that I get that week's outcome done, and therefore meet that milestone? Let me give you an example for this train of thought:

Let's say that my **goal** is to study all the basic sciences for a big exam in med school. This entails about eight different topics, so those will be the milestones.

Next question, what **milestone** am I working on this month (January)? I'll be studying Anatomy.

Next, what **outcome** can I produce *this week* that will get me closer to that milestone? The first week of January, I will read and take notes on all of the review material on Anatomy.

Finally, what **routine** will I implement to ensure I have the time to get that task done? I will study for five hours in the morning and three hours in the afternoon every day.

Perfect! That wasn't so hard, was it? Alright, now it's your turn. Take out your journal and do this for one of your Ladder Goals.

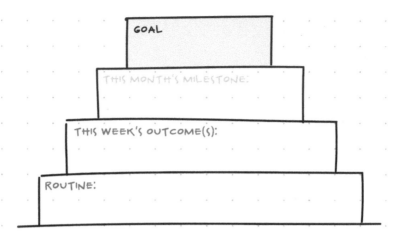

GETTING STARTED WITH YOUR GOAL

Yes, I know that so far, we've planned only one week, and that is nowhere close to planning out our "entire" project. Don't worry, we'll get there! Before we continue, though, I would like to give you a piece of advice. If you're not too familiar with planning long term, assign a milestone to an already defined time frame, like a week or month. The beginning and end of a week or month are very clear and are dates that you will most likely be aware of. This means that you'll have a clear starting point and finish line for your milestones or weekly outcomes. It'll just make your life so much easier. For example, as of right now, I'm writing a chapter (outcome) per week (timeframe). Some chapters take me four days, and others take me ten. However, when I'm making my plans, I assign one chapter to each week simply because it's easier. If I happen to finish before the deadline, I can start working on the next one, and if I'm late, I can rearrange my plans. The point is, don't go crazy planning for specific number of days. Stick to weeks and months so your map is not overly complicated.

Of course, rearranging your plans is going to depend on the flexibility of that deadline. Your personal projects are more likely to be able to be postponed, whereas the projects pertaining your job or school have an external deadline that can't be moved. The more you do this, the easier it'll be to judge how much time you should assign to each milestone.

THE SPREAD

Now, it's time to take it a step further. We'll use the same train of thought to plan a little further into the future. Let's start filling the Milestone Map. Remember that the objective is to end up with actions or tasks that you can actually work on. Of course, there are many ways on how to create this spread in your journal, but for now, I'll share the most basic format. Once you're comfortable with it, you can design your own however you'd like. This is what a Milestone Map looks like:

GOAL: BIG EXAM	MONTHLY MILESTONE	WEEKLY OUTCOMES	ROUTINE
	JANUARY	1 read/notes subject	
DUE: July 30th	STUDY ALL OF ANATOMY	2 study textbook	
		3 anatomy questions	
WHY: Important for my medical career		4 review weak topics	
	FEBRUARY	5 notes + study p.1-100	read 20 pages, break, then study what I read for the day
MILESTONES:	STUDY ALL OF PHYSIOLOGY	6 notes + study p.100-200	
• Anatomy		7 notes + study p.200-300	
• Physiology		8 review questions	study 6 hours a day
• Biochemistry			
• Pathology			
• Microbiology	MARCH	9	
• Pharmacology		10	
• Embryology		11	
• Ethics		12	

On the left side of this spread, there's a space for you to write in the goal, the due date, and the why behind your goal as well as a list of the milestones you came up with. This example walks you through three months of a project. Each row represents one month. At the top, there's a space for you to write what milestone(s) you'll be working on that month. Next to that, there's a list of the weeks (labeled with their corresponding numbers) for each of the weeks in that month. This is where you write the outcomes you wish to produce that week that will get your closer to the completing the milestone. On the third column, there's a space for you to write the routine or set of tasks to get done in order to produce those outcomes.

Wait! Before you go crazy filling every single one of these spaces, remember that life is messy. You have absolutely no clue what can happen in three months, so filling in week #11 now with something that could completely change in the future is useless. Right? No! Well, yes and no. Yes, because it could change and no because it'll give you an idea of when you'll accomplish that and if that's enough time to meet your deadline. So, how do we solve this issue? Post-its! If we're being real, whatever you wrote in for week #9 will probably change, but most likely that task still needs to get done. If it's on a Post-it, you can simply migrate it to the following space or wherever it goes. I limit myself to filling in only some of the spaces, usually the monthly milestones, with a general idea of what I want to be working on that month. This way, I can easily rearrange them if I need to.

For Pros: If you feel comfortable with the planning process, you can add multiple outcomes to produce in one week or multiple milestones in one month. I try to keep my map as simple as possible, but there are some cases where this may be necessary. Anyway, just make sure you're not overestimating the amount of work you can get done in a week and remember to add some wiggle room.

Well...It's time to fill in your Milestone Map! Go as far into the future as you feel comfortable with. Remember that not every space has to be filled. This is a dynamic spread in your journal, and you can make as many changes as you see fit. Let me show you how I'd fill in Sam's Milestone Map if I was planning ahead for her Ladder Goal.

GOAL: LAUNCH A BLOG ON JUNE 1ST

APRIL: W

JANUARY: BRANDING & RESEARCH

Week 1: Brand indentity
Week 2: Create logo + Brand aesthetic.
Week 3: Research tools (website, apps, photos)
Week 4: Research skills (marketing, writing)

Routine: Work for 1-2 hrs on weeknights, after work.

MAY: LAS

FEBRUARY: BUILD THE WEBSITE

Routine: Work for 1-2 hrs on weeknights, after work.

MARCH: BRAINSTORM & PLAN

Week 8: Research similar blogs.
Week 9: Come up with 10 ideas for potential blog posts + outlines
Week 10 & 11: Experiment and find the best time to write within my schedule and writing goal per week.

Routine: Work at night, after dinner.

NOTES:

GET STARTED WITH YOUR LADDER GOAL

Use this template to plan in Milestone Map style the first two months of this goal. Good Luck! And remember, it's okay for the plan to change, this is just an outline.

GOAL:

DUE:
WHY:

MILESTONES:

MONTHLY MILESTONE

WEEKLY OUTCOME

ROUTINE

Once you get comfortable with the concept behind the Milestone Map, you can play around with the format as much as you like! For the sake of fun, here are some other ideas on creating these spreads in case you're looking for inspiration.

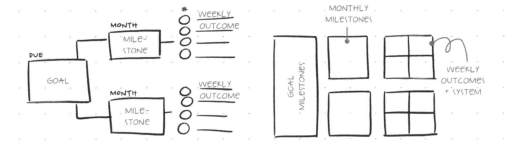

NEXT LEVEL

If you're not a planner at heart, this is probably enough information for you to get a better handle on your long term projects. You can refer to this spread whenever you want or need to work on your project. I advise you to revise it as often as possible. If you are a journaling junkie like me, however, or you wish to stay on top of your goal and maybe work on it on a daily or weekly basis, keep reading!

The idea behind creating a Milestone Map that breaks your Ladder Goals down to weekly outcomes and even routines is that you'll be able to incorporate working on this project into your existing lifestyle. The way I do this is by referring back to this spread at least once a week during my Weekly Check-In. During this session, I take the time to figure out what part of my project, or what outcomes, I'll be working on the following week. This way, I make sure I'm staying on track.

Brief pause here. Just wanted to say that if you choose not to work on your project for that week, or few weeks, that's totally fine. The point is that you are making a conscious choice of where you'll be spending your time in the following week, and that you are always aware of where you're at in your project.

Back to taking this to the next level: Once I know what I want to be working on and my Milestone Map is up to date—which, may I mention, takes no more than five minutes—I transfer this information into my Weekly Board just so that it's right there, staring at me. If you'll recall, the Weekly Board is where I outline the game plan for the upcoming week.

So, under the "goals" space, I write in the milestones or weekly outcomes that I hope to accomplish that week for all my Ladder Goals (which is usually just one). This way, as I'm planning and working through my week, I have a reminder that the project is something I need to work on. It doesn't get lost in between all the other more menial tasks, and I know I need to prioritize this time as much as I can. This is how I conquer my goals. How will you conquer yours?

CHAPTER 10

The Magic Is in Your Habits

Who you are is a reflection of your habits. As James Clear, the author of *Atomic Habits*, put it:

> "Your outcomes are a lagging measure of your habits. Your net worth is a lagging measure of your financial habits. Your weight is a lagging measure of your eating habits. Your knowledge is a lagging measure of your learning habits. Your clutter is a lagging measure of your cleaning habits. You get what you repeat."

In other words, you are a compilation of all the tiny habits you've created. Whether they are conscious habits or unconscious ones, they define who you are. The good news is this: you can choose your habits. You have the power to change the unproductive ones, to set up new ones, and to reinvent the kind of person you want to be.

Habits are the key towards a specific identity you are trying to build. I've said before that you reach your goals by putting in consistent effort towards that goal. Well, building habits, by definition, is turning an action into something that happens on a regular basis. Building strong, carefully chosen habits is how you reach your goals. This is the answer you've been looking for. This is how you become who you want to be.

> *"We are what we repeatedly do. Excellence, then, is not an act, but a habit."*
>
> —*Aristotle*

All the stuff we did before—defining what you want out of life, turning that into a perfectly constructed goal statement, breaking that down into a plan that will ensure you accomplish that goal—is worthless if you can't invest the time and effort needed. One way to hack the self-discipline it takes to choose to work on your goals is to develop a habit, so that there is no choice, the action just happens automatically.

Your Current Goals, in case you need a reminder, are the things you want more or less of at this moment in your life. Things like: read more, go to sleep earlier, drink more water, eat less junk food, run more often, etc. These are the things that, if they become part of your lifestyle, they will shape who you are. For these kinds of goals, you must create a **system, routine, or rule** that will allow you to stay on track. In other words, you have to build a habit that will allow you to become the kind of person who "reads" or "runs" or "takes care of their body" or whatever your goal is.

Even reaching your Ladder Goals depends on your habits. Of course, that entails more planning and milestones to give your direction, boost your motivation, and ensure that you're moving at the right pace, but in the end, it boils down to a system or routine that will allow you to work on that goal consistently.

In the end, who you are is a result of your daily actions, the small choices that seem insignificant at the moment, yet add up to your identity. So, when it comes to what produces real, tangible results, the answer is not your goals, but your habits because these are what will ensure that you show up, regardless of the motivation you might be feeling in that moment.

> *"You don't rise to the level of your goals. You fall to the level of your systems."*
>
> —James Clear

WHAT ARE HABITS?

According to the five dictionaries I consulted to make sure I got this right, a habit is "an acquired behavior pattern regularly followed until it has become almost involuntary," the three key concepts being *acquired, regular* and *automatic*. **Acquired:** meaning that it wasn't always a habit, which in turn means that you have the ability to build new ones. **Regular:** meaning that it must be repeated consistently in order for it to become a habit. **Automatic:** which means that eventually, once the habit is formed, the action will be performed without having to actively choose to do it, you'll just do it "out of habit."

THE HABIT LOOP

In his book *The Power of Habit*, Charles Duhigg explains the concept of the Habit Loop, the three-step process that governs any habit. First there is a **cue**, "a trigger that tells your brain to go into automatic mode and which habit to use." Then, the **routine** is performed, the action or thought that follows that cue. Finally, there is a **reward**, which is the result you get from performing the routine. The purpose of the reward is to help your brain identify if this loop is worth repeating or not. The better the reward, the likelier it is you'll repeat this routine when the specific cue shows up.

This can be applied to pretty much anything. Cue: see phone. Routine: open social media. Reward: entertainment, instant gratification. Cue: see to-do list. Routine: tackle first task. Reward: I get to cross off that task.

Later in his book, Duhigg explains an addition to The Habit Loop, called **craving**. He explains that as you consistently go through the loop, you start craving the reward. The more you repeat it, the earlier within the loop you'll crave it, until eventually, you'll crave the reward as soon as you see the cue. This is what allows us to keep repeating these loops and therefore, form a habit.

The reason why this knowledge is so important is because now you can create the cues that you might need in your life to perform the routines you wish to establish. Or, you can add rewards where you see fit so you'll be motivated to perform the habit. Knowing this allows you to tailor these loops into something that triggers you to stick to your habits.

HOW TO BUILD HABITS

I learned about habits from one of the most disciplined people I have ever known, my Grandma. I remember after sleepovers at her house, she would take us to the kitchen and pour herself a glass of warm water with lemon. When we asked why she said she simply did that every single morning, along with a really long explanation of the benefits of it, she also told us that she washed her dishes right after she used them and she would go to bed every night at the same exact time. She'd say, *"Todo en la vida es un hábito,"* which means, everything in life is a habit. She always seemed so put together and full of wisdom. I remember being amazed by that level of discipline. So naturally, I tried the lemon water in the morning thing in high school. Yeah... that lasted about two weeks. I found it so hard to stick to that "habit." In retrospect, I didn't realize that at that very same time, I was making my own bed every morning before school, which is also a habit. Fast forward ten years, I drink lemon water every morning. What changed? My systems.

See, sticking to a habit you've already built is a piece of cake. Which is why after ten years of making my bed every morning, it was easy for me to keep doing so in college without my mom checking up on me. By the way, thanks for forcing me to do so when I was little, mom, *"valió la pena."* (It was worth it!) Sticking to habits you are trying to build, however, is not nearly as easy. In fact, it's quite hard. It requires so much discipline and so much willpower. Or, a little discipline, a little willpower, and a very good system. Your choice.

WHAT I WISH I KNEW

Whether you are able to stick to a habit or not depends much more on the systems you set up than on your own self-discipline. Of course, there is so much more information regarding this topic, entire books even, but out of the things I've read and learned, there are a few bits of advice that are essential to getting started. The following are the things I wish I knew when I started building habits.

DEFINE THE CUES

Figure out what the cue for your habit will be, and make sure it's staring right at you. For example, let's say you want to get into the habit of taking your vitamins. If you leave it to chance, odds are, you'll forget to take them. Instead, *decide* the cue. This could be an alarm on your phone, a reminder, or simply leaving the vitamin bottle on the kitchen counter (cue: seeing the bottle). Without a clear, consistent cue, there will be no routine.

INCORPORATE YOUR HABIT INTO YOUR EXISTING ROUTINES

Whenever possible, try to tie in the habit with a routine in your existing lifestyle and the things that you do every day. For example, at some point, I wanted to listen to more podcasts. So, I tried to figure out at what parts of my routine I could attach this too. As a result, I now listen to a podcast every morning while I'm getting ready and commuting to the hospital. When my friend wanted to work out more, I told her to try wearing the gym clothes to school (or taking them) and to go straight from her last class to the school's gym, so her school routine didn't end until *after* she went to the gym.

THE TWO-MINUTE RULE

This is concept that I learned from James Clear's *Atomic Habits*. It suggests that in the beginning, you should scale a habit down so that it only takes two minutes or less to perform. For example, instead of "Read fifteen minutes a day," you could start with "Read one page per day." This allows you to show up every day, no matter what. This is exactly what I did with my reading habit. I decided that I wanted to read before bed. In the beginning, I had to constantly remind myself to take my Kindle to the bedroom. Some days, I read for twenty minutes, others, I read a paragraph. The point is that no matter what, I was reading *something* before bed. Now, I don't even have to think about taking my Kindle to bed, it's just a habit. And, I'm starting to believe that I'm "the kind of person who reads before bed." Reading something is better than not reading at all because you are still doing it on a regular basis. Once it becomes a habit, you can expand on it.

YOUR ENVIRONMENT AND THE TWENTY SECOND RULE

Although you may not be aware of it, your surroundings determine a lot of your choices and actions. They either motivate or discourage you to stick to your goals, so whenever possible, tailor your environment to incite positive action. One easy way to apply this is by using the Twenty Second Rule, a concept introduced by Shawn Achor in his book *The Happiness Advantage*. The rule dictates that you should reduce the amount of time it takes to get into a positive habit to, hopefully, less than twenty seconds. For example, let's say you want to practice playing the keyboard more. If it's stored in some corner of your closet inside its box, and every time you want to use it you have to build the stand and the whole set-up, chances are, you won't do it as often. Instead, if you have everything already set up so that whenever you decide to practice, all you have to so it sit down and start playing, you're much more likely to stick to your habit.

THE FOUR LAWS OF BEHAVIOR CHANGE

Clear presents in his book the theory that in order to incite behavior change you should build your habits following these four rules. One, make it obvious. In other words, make the cue easily recognizable. Two, make it attractive. Three, make it easy, meaning, make sure that it's simple and convenient to get into the habit. Four, make is satisfying. Make sure it has a reward, so you're more likely to repeat it. In contrast, when you are trying to quit a bad habit, apply the inverse of each rule. Make it invisible, unattractive, difficult, and unsatisfying.

TRACK YOUR PROGRESS

The final, most important piece of advice I wish I knew was the importance of tracking my progress. Tracking your goals will improve your chances of achieving them. It's that simple. According to the American Psychological Association, "prompting progress monitoring improves behavioral performance and the likelihood of attaining one's goals." The studies that were analyzed focused mainly on personal health goals such as losing weight, quitting smoking, changing diet, or lowering blood pressure—very common goals! The results stated that monitoring progress towards the outcome does, in fact, increase the likelihood of achieving that outcome. That seems like an easy enough hack to make sure I follow through with my goals.

If you look at a calendar marked with an X for every time you stuck to your habits, you'll immediately be motivated to keep going. You can leverage Jerry Seinfeld's "Don't Break The Chain" strategy. The idea is that if you do something every single day, you can see a chain of "X" on a calendar and you'll be motivated to not break the chain. The same applies for when you see progress in a chart or a graph. If you see a positive trend, your brain automatically fills in the future data points. Charts, graphs, and trackers slowly prove to you that your small efforts are piling up and that you are actually capable of achieving your goal. You build *self-efficacy.* This is the belief in your capacity to execute a certain behavior necessary to produce specific performance attainments. In other words, it's basically your self-confidence pertaining to a certain task. One of the sources of self-efficacy is experience. The more you *see* that you are actually sticking to your habit, the more you convince yourself that you are capable of doing so in the long run, and the more you adopt that identity. This is especially important when it comes to big, life-changing habits like eating healthy, exercising, achieving deep work every day, or waking up early. The key, however, for you to believe in yourself is the evidence. You can produce this evidence by simply tracking your progress.

Another great advantage of tracking your progress, one that really works for me, actually, is that it creates a tiny reward at the end of the habit loop. What I mean is that when you perform a habit, you get to cross it off on your tracker, which gives you a little dose of satisfaction. So small, yet so powerful. There have been so many times I've done a habit just because I wanted to cross it off or I didn't want to break my streak.

When I said "simply tracking your progress," I really meant *simple.* You don't have to create an overwhelmingly complicated chart with tons of data points and millions of habits to track. In my opinion, the simpler, the better. At least, when you're getting started. Before I go on, I do have to say that if you must, you can track your habits in an app. There are many options out there, and I'm sure you can find the one that works for you. Make sure that it provides a visual of your streak. If you prefer the analog experience, however, let's talk "habit trackers."

THE BULLET JOURNAL COMMUNITY'S MISCONCEPTION

A habit tracker is, in essence, a "chart" with the list of habits on one axis and the days of the week/month/year on the other. Every time you complete a habit, you mark the corresponding box as completed. Simple, right?

HABIT TRACKER

	M	T	W	T	F	S	S
read							
workout							
vitamins							
journal							

More often than not, I see "habit trackers" that have twenty plus habits listed, that end up half-filled, and for which the habits are completely different the following month. I've been guilty of this in the past. I think part of it might be the Busy Identity or the idea that the more habits we "fill in," the more disciplined we are. But these aren't habits, these are just things you are doing on a regular-ish basis during that month. If they were habits, you'd be trying to stick to them until they become *habitual*. With this oversimplification of what habits are and overestimation of how many we can actually build at the same time, we've diminished the power of habits. It seems as if habits are these menial five-minute actions that we'd like to try out, when in reality, they are the building blocks of the person you are trying to become. They deserve more attention and more significance in your life, and therefore, in your journal. This is why I urge you to reduce your list of "habits" to a few you will really focus on so you have the time and motivation to actually stick to them. The idea of tracking them is not so you can fill in the box, but rather so that you can become the kind of person who does that habit on a regular basis. The goal is to get to the point where you don't even need to track it anymore because it's become automatic.

Remember that you're not including habits just because some "influencer" you love said they do this every day. There has to be a reason and a goal behind every habit you bring into your life. Start by tracking the habits you came up with for your Current Goals and the routine you set up in your Milestone Map. That's more than enough to get started.

FORMAT MANIA

Most habit trackers are created for a set of "monthly" habits, so thirty or thirty-one boxes to mark the completion of each habit. This is great for people who don't have a hard time referencing this page in their journal and come back to it on a regular basis. I also like this format because it paints a bigger picture of how consistently you're keeping up with those actions. However, you can also track your habits on a weekly habit tracker (up to seven boxes) and include this tracker in your Weekly Board. This, I believe, might make it easier to stick to those habits, especially at the beginning, because your actions will be right next to your task lists. Finally, you can, of course, also create a tracker for a couple of months or even the entire year. This would be ideal for a habit that you already have in place, and you simply want to track it "for fun," but not so much for a habit that you are trying to build. In my opinion, a yearly tracker is too big of a commitment and therefore more daunting than motivating. I suggest you experiment with the length and pick the one that works best for you. You can always switch it up.

Aside from the time frame you assign, a habit tracker can have many formats. This is where it gets fun! I'll go over their pros and cons, so you get to choose the format that is more convenient for you at any given time. Again, do you.

GRID FORMAT

This is the standard and most common habit tracker format. It's a table with the habits as rows and the days of the month as columns, or vice versa.

	1	2	3	4	5	6	7	8	9	10	11	12	13	14	15
MAKE THE BED	x	x	x	x	x	x	x	x	x		x	x	x	x	x
SKINCARE	x	x	x	x	x		x	x			x		x		
READ 15 MINUTES	x	x		x	x		x	x	x	x	x		x	x	
TAKE VITAMINS	x	x	x		x	x	x		x		x	x		x	x
MORNING YOGA	x	x	x	x	x	x	x	x	x		x	x	x	x	x

This habit tracker allows you to see patterns for a specific day. For example, on Fridays you always miss your habits, or on January 15, you had an incredibly busy day and couldn't do any of your habits. It allows you to spot patterns which makes it easier to modify your behavior in the future. For example, you could simply decide that on Fridays, you won't do your actions because they don't fit your intentions or your schedule. I love that this habit tracker is incredibly easy and quick to set up, it's minimalist and you only have to set it up once at the beginning of the month. So, it's quite convenient if you're on a time crunch.

MINI-CALENDARS

This one is definitely aesthetically pleasing, in my humble opinion. However, it does take a bunch of time and effort to set up. In this format, each habit gets its own mini-calendar, so you can cross out the dates when your action got done. Because you have to create so many mini-calendars, I suggest you use this format only if you have very few habits to track. It has the advantage of really letting you focus on one specific goal and providing a very clear visual of your progress towards that goal.

Magic Trick: Don't write the dates, just draw the squares!

CATEGORIES & TIME ZONES

This format is like the grid format, except that you group your habits by categories. This is ideal for a person who has many things to do in their day and maybe for people who have many categories in their lives to take care of in a daily basis. I don't encourage you to use this format if you aren't used to tracking your habits yet because it can get very overwhelming to see so many empty boxes to fill. This has the advantage that it lets you see what category or area in your life you might be having a hard time with, or which ones you are nailing!

Personally, I only use this kind of tracker when I am building new morning and evening routines. I use it to track all the steps in my morning routine so I can get used to it very quickly and tweak it as I see fit. I'll split the table up into "morning," "evening," and "habits." Having everything in one place makes my life so much simpler.

HABITS

	1	2	3	4	5	6	7	8	9	...
MAKE THE BED	x	x	x	x	x	x	x	x	x	
SKINCARE	x	x	x	x	x	x	x	x	x	
VITAMINS	x	x	x	x	x	x	x	x	x	
JOURNAL	x	x	x	x	x	x	x	x	x	
STRETCH	x	x	x	x	x	x	x	x	x	
EVENING REVIEW	x	x	x	x	x	x	x	x	x	
MISE EN PLACE	x	x	x	x	x	x	x	x	x	
SKINCARE	x	x	x	x	x	x	x	x	x	
TIDY	x	x	x	x	x	x	x	x	x	
READ 15 MIN	x	x	x	x	x	x	x	x	x	
MEDITATE	x	x	x	x	x	x	x	x	x	
PRACTICE GUITAR	x	x	x	x	x	x	x	x	x	

MORNING HABITS
(MORNING ROUTINE)

EVENING HABITS
(EVENING ROUTINE)

OTHER HABITS
(DO ANY TIME; NOT
PART OF A ROUTINE)

Of course, there are tons of different formats you can play around with and lots of room for creativity. This is just the skeleton for any habit tracker. And, in reality, that's what matters the most. The rest is fluff.

THE "SKIPPED" ICON

Like I mentioned earlier, looking at a perfect chain will spike your motivation to keep it going. But sometimes, life happens, and skipping that habit is completely out of your control. Now, that doesn't mean you should lose your streak. Right? For this, I suggest you come up with an icon or symbol that illustrates "skipped," meaning you couldn't follow through because of an external situation. This will allow just enough flexibility for you to not get discouraged by the missing X on the calendar. But please, be honest with yourself. "I couldn't stop binging my Netflix show" is not a valid reason to skip, right?

THE NOTES SECTION

Last quick tip: From years of experience, I can tell you that the most important section of any habit tracker or tracking app is the "notes" section. This is just a space within your spread where you can write notes about your progress as you fill in your tracker or as you miss days. In the beginning, you won't know what to write, and that's fine. As you become more comfortable with the system, you'll see that this is where you'll find the tiny details that you need to adjust in order to nail your habits. For example, in one of my trackers, I wrote: *I haven't been able to keep up with my meditation habit because I don't have a specific time of the day to meditate.* From this, I learned that I needed a better cue for my meditation practice, and, of course, a time to do it! When I finally altered my routine to include meditation and added an alarm on my phone as the cue, I was able to stick to my habit. So, just write whatever notes come to your mind. Most of them will be useless, but the very few that aren't are extremely valuable. This is where you'll find how to hack your habits.

> *"What gets measured, gets managed."*
>
> —Peter Ducker

I absolutely love this quote because it's so true. Tracking your behavior, more than motivating you, allows you to modify it. How can you change what you do if you don't *know what* you do? This can be applied to anything. In order for you to improve on any area of your life or any habit you've already adopted, you need to know where to start and what to change. You need to identify the base level. You need to see your progress. Then you can choose how to modify it, and from there, how to grow. This is where reviewing your progress and your goals comes in.

CHAPTER 11

Review, Review, Review.

How many Decembers have you looked back at your resolutions from the beginning of the year and asked yourself: "Was that even one of my goals?" Don't worry, it happens to all of us. You might change your mind about a certain goal midyear or lose interest in this goal altogether. You might realize that this goal is no longer relevant to your life, or that you no longer enjoy or need it. That's okay.

Adapting to your changing life is part of the growth process. It's okay to change your mind. Don't ever let your goals restrict you. However, if you *forgot* that you even set up that goal for yourself in the first place, well, that's not great. Nobody wants that. The good news is that it's easy to fix! How do we avoid a year going by without ever so much as reading our goals? Create a routine, a system. Create a space in your calendar for you to review your goals on a regular basis. It can be as simple as this: the last weekend of every month, I'll read my goals, or every week, I'll rewrite my goals, or every Monday, I'll text them to my best friend. It doesn't have to take long and it doesn't have to be fancy as long as it helps remind you what you are working for.

This is what Airing Your Ambitions, the fourth step in planning your goals, is all about. Keep your goals out in the open, where they can motivate you. Track them. And, every once in a while, reevaluate them.

The sky is the limit when it comes to putting your goals out into the world. It can be as simple as having them on a Post-it on your bathroom mirror, or like me, on the wall in front of my desk. You can text them to a friend, rewrite them every morning, set them as your desktop picture or phone lock screen, yell them every morning, or announce them on social media every once in a while. Or, like we talked about before, reflect on them in your Weekly Recap. It's completely up to you, but it's crucial that you find a way to be reminded of your goals on a regular basis. This will probably change over time. Find what works for you. My current system: If I have the time, I rewrite my monthly goals every morning, recap them at the end of every week, and have designated space for the weekly outcomes I'll be working on in my Weekly Board. At the end of the month. I review the overall progress on my goals. No, I don't always do *all* of that. For the most part, though, making sure that working towards my professional or personal goals every day is what allows me to stay motivated and on track.

THE MONTHLY REVIEW: REEVALUATING YOUR GOALS

What is the use of tracking your progress if you're not going to do anything with that information? The whole point of monitoring your progress is so you to take a step back and analyze your behavior. I don't mean an extremely complicated analysis and perfectly crafted résumé of what you've been up to. I just mean a small designated time in which you reflect a little on your goals and your progress. It can be as simple as you want it to be. In fact, the simpler, the better. The idea is to decide how you will move forward with each of your goals. Will you keep pursuing this goal and its "daily" actions? Will you put it on pause? Or, will you let it go? It's as simple as that, and if that's all you can do right now to evaluate your goals, that's fine. That's great! All that matters is that you took a moment to make a conscious decision about your future behavior. All the details come later with experience and practice.

WHEN?

The most important routine you have to set in place is that of reevaluating your goals. When are you going to do this? At the end of the week? End of the month? Mid-week? Every three months? Every night? It doesn't matter how often it is, it matters that you do it and that it fits your schedule. My rule of thumb is at least once a month. Just take a moment to remind yourself what your goals are and how you wish to pursue them the following month. Ten minutes will do to get started.

WHAT?

What you're looking for is consistency in completing your habits. Focus on finding the progress from one month to the other. Tali Sharot, a professor of cognitive neuroscience, explains in her TED Talk "How to Motivate Yourself to Change Your Behavior" that the most effective form of progress monitoring is highlighting the progress, not the decline. That is because our brain does a really good job at processing positive information about the future, and, of course, a really bad job of processing the negative information. Don't let the empty spaces of your habit tracker cloud the big picture. You are moving forward no matter how small the steps! Try to highlight the positive information by focusing on the marked boxes and the goals you are actually seeing progress in. What were your wins?

HOW?

Look for the details! Once you've given yourself a pat in the back, can you try to identify what is causing your failures or missed days on the tracker? What things cause friction? What's getting in the way of you sticking to your habits? If you can, try to do something to change that the following month. If you're having trouble with one specific habit, think back to the Habit Loop or the rules we talked about before and see what adjustments you can make to hack your behavior. Work on one thing at a time. Don't overwhelm yourself by reaching for perfect. Try to answer the question: How can I modify my behavior in order to reach this goal?

MONTHLY REFLECTION

✔ MONTHLY FOCUS/PRIORITY

Did I prioritize this on a regular basis?
Was I able to achieve it?

✔ MONTH'S WINS

What things am I proud of this month?

✔ WHAT WORKED / WHAT DIDN'T?

What little things in my routine or daily life worked or
didn't really work for me? How can I improve them?

✔ REVIEW EACH GOAL

Did I acheive it?
Did my approach/actions work? If not, what can I do
to make sure I achieve it next month?
Is this worth pursuing in the future?

✔ ONE POSITIVE LESSON

How did I grow this month?

Now it's time to define your own review questions. Feel free to use mine for inspiration!

MONTHLY REFLECTION

Think about how you want to reflect on your progress.
Create 3-5 questions you can work through at the end of each month.

✔

✔

✔

✔

✔

BONUS: GOALS MASTERMIND

Sometimes it's simple and you don't need a lot of planning. At other times, however, you need a bit more direction on how working towards your goals will play into your life. For these moments, I created the Goals Mastermind. It's a simple spread to summarize the concepts we've talked about in the last few chapters. It's not something you have to do every month, but it can help give you a lot of direction if you feel like you might need it.

goals mastermind

WHY	GOAL	ACTIONS	DETAILS
Why do you want to achieve this goal? Why does this matter?	What do you wish to accomplish? What kind of person do you want to be?	What can you do on a regular basis to get you closer to this goal?	How are you going to do this? When? What do you need?
Learn from experts	Read one book in April	Read everyday	Read 30 minutes before bed
Learn to manage my money and save	Budget and Track Expenses	Monthly budget and Monthly expenses	Plan budget at the beginning of the month. Input weekly expenses every Friday. Summary (end of the month)

It's basically another version of the Battle Blueprint. For every goal, you'll write the why behind it on the first column, the goal statement on the second, the habits/actions/routines/rules that will allow you to achieve it in the third column, and finally, in the last column, the details of how you'll make this happen. This last column is where you design how you'll actually stick to that habit. For example, let's say I want to read more.

Why: I want to learn more from experts.

Goal: Read one book in April.

Habit: Read every day.

Details: Go to bed thirty minutes before my bedtime with nothing but my book. Read until I fall asleep.

WHY

GOAL

ACTIONS

DETAILS

goals mastermind

Not everyone needs this level of detail, but if you're feeling lost more often than not, you can use this to nail down your routines and what you're supposed to be working on at this moment. I especially love using this spread at the beginning of a busy month to lay out what my life will look like the next few weeks. Again, stick to few goals to avoid getting overwhelmed.

WORDS OF ADVICE

LESS IS MORE

Start with a few goals, practice following through, and build up from there. Being overwhelmed by the number of things you have to get done will get you nowhere, so start small, and before you know it, you'll be a pro at building new habits!

It's much more effective to work on one habit per month and actually nail it than to work on seven and not build any of them. I limit myself to working on *one* Ladder Goal at a time and maybe a few other Current Goals. At most, I'm building three habits at a time. But that's just what works for me. Find your perfect challenge.

THE MYTH OF A FILLED HABIT TRACKER

Trust me when I say a completely filled habit tracker does not exist. We are human, life happens, and not completing your actions for a few days of the month is okay. In fact, I've been tracking my habits for a couple of years now, and I think I have *never* filled an entire habit tracker. Focus on the good, not the empty spaces! Don't think of the tracker as boxes to cross off, but as a space for you to tally the amount of times you completed the habit.

THE DIGITAL SUPPORT SYSTEM

I'll be the first to admit that there is a huge advantage of using digital tools for all the things we've talked about so far. Nonetheless, if analog habit tracking is not enough for you, don't be afraid to merge the digital and analog worlds. Keeping a habit tracker on your phone allows you to immediately tick off a habit when you've completed it, which creates that immediate satisfaction that we talked about earlier. For me, reviewing progress on my goals and habits, though, is just not good enough in an app. So, I keep track of my habits in my dot journal. I keep a spread with one month's habits, with one of the formats that we discussed in the previous chapter. This is where I also write out my thoughts, notes on my failures, ideas for the upcoming month, and where I monitor my progress. This visual representation is just something I need. Find the best fit for you, and never be afraid to make the best of both worlds.

LET IT GO

Some people believe that because something is on their habit tracker or their goal list, they are forced to stick with it until...? It's okay to stop doing something that no longer serves you, that you no longer enjoy, or that you simply don't want to pursue any more. Tracking your progress is more of a recollection of information rather than a strict list of to-dos. So, when you are reevaluating your goal and habits, remember that it's okay to stop. Be honest with yourself.

YOUR TURN

Working on your goals and your personal dreams is a much bigger topic than four chapters of a book, but hopefully, this is enough to get you started. Remember that it's a journey with hills of immense motivation and valleys of complete inaction. It's okay, it happens to all of us. What matters is how you keep going. How you readjust your behavior. That's why having the evidence right in front of you is so powerful. You have all the tools you need, now it's just a matter of trial and error. I always thought about goals and dreamed about things I wanted to do in my life, but it wasn't until I started journaling that I found a way to make them happen and to keep working towards the life I imagine for myself. It's wild how an empty notebook, a good pen, and a little creativity can completely change your life. Are you ready for the magic?

PART IV

Creating Rituals for Success

CHAPTER 12

Rise and Shine

O h, the morning routine...this is one of my many obsessions. A few years ago, I made it my life's mission to create the perfect morning routine. Well, *my* perfect morning routine. Keep in mind that I was a fourth-year medical student at the time; required to be at the hospital at 7:00 a.m. sharp—even though the doctors usually got there around 8:00—possibly sleep deprived and definitely buried in tons of unread textbook pages. In that moment, creating a morning routine seemed trivial, yet a great excuse to focus on something "productive" that wasn't studying. You know those things you do to pretend you're getting stuff done, but really you're just procrastinating? Yep, something like that. In retrospect, I was starting a journey that would very drastically change my life.

Anyway, I read books for inspiration, did my research on the best morning practices, watched every "Morning Routine" vlog available on YouTube, grabbed my current journal, and made a list of the things I wanted to include in my morning routine. It turned out to be quite long, as you would expect. After a few weeks of trying, and failing, to do these things in the morning, I gave up on my goal and went on with my life. I didn't have a purpose. It wasn't until I found myself distracted most of the day, with lack of motivation, sleep deprivation, and in total Reactive Mode, that I sat down one night and created the perfect morning routine, one that would increase my productivity and motivate me to get my life together, one that would gear me into Proactive Mode. This is what you will create in this chapter, a morning routine that *fuels* your productivity.

There are a million things you could prioritize in the morning and a million kinds of routines you could create. My favorite kind, however, is a morning routine that leaves me inspired to take control of my day, one that builds that productive momentum. It's widely known that the way we begin our day has tremendous impact on how the rest of the day seems to go. That daily productivity is something we all want in our lives, and having a morning routine can also have a huge impact in your life in the long run.

WHY YOU NEED A MORNING ROUTINE

"You must come up with a morning routine you do more mornings than not, that puts you in control of yourself and in control of your day."

—*Mel Robbins*

It's common knowledge that many highly successful people have very tailored and specific morning routines, but what is success, really? Money? Great job? Happy family? Health? Tons of memories? Gorgeous Instagram feed? Fame? Influence? Anything that is popping through your head now? Who's to say that the life you have right now is not a successful one already? You know, even without a morning routine in it! The premise that having a morning routine is essential to create success, although arguably true, is not encouraging enough. A morning routine will not guarantee you success, but it could bring you direction, inspiration, mental clarity, emotional balance, physical health, a productive mindset, freedom to work on the things that matter, and even the motivation to go after your dream life. A morning routine is more than just a hack to success (by no means is it a shortcut); it's a lifestyle, one in which you prioritize yourself, your goals, and your health over the hustle of a busy life. You don't need a morning routine to be happy, or to be successful, or even to be productive; but it will make achieving those things so much easier. It's about shifting your mindset. It's a life choice, because believe me, it will change your life. At least, it dramatically changed mine.

"One of the commonalities that you spot very quickly when you interview hundreds of world class performers is that they all have consistent morning routines."

—Tim Ferriss

The way you wake up in the morning, your mood, your energy, and the first decisions you make sets the tone for the rest of the day. The more small tasks you accomplish, the more you convince yourself you can keep accomplishing tasks the rest of the day. This results in a more intentional, productive day.

When you decide that mornings are a time to work on yourself and your goals, whatever those may be, there will always be a specific time of the day, an empty slot in your calendar, in which you can work on those important things that you might otherwise dismiss. Have you ever thought, "Today, I'm going to start working on that project that I've been wanting to start for a month," then the day goes by and you keep postponing it because more urgent things keep coming up? By the end of the day, you are so tired that you move it to the weekend or whenever you "have more time." Well, now you have no excuse. Aside from the fact that you've learned to prioritize for these goals, by including them in you morning routine, you'll always have a designated time to work on them.

Whether it is for an hour or fifteen minutes, a morning routine provides that space where you can take action on those long-term goals you keep postponing.

If you do a set of activities in a similar order, at the same time, on a regular basis, they will eventually become a habit; and isn't it just so much easier when those things you might not love to do, but are very good for you, become habits? Wouldn't you just love to wake up and almost without even thinking about it go work out...oh, I wish! It's. So. Hard. Can you tell how much working out isn't my thing? By having these habits and structure in place, you decrease decision fatigue. This is the idea that throughout the day the quality of your decisions decreases because you become more and more "tired" of making decisions. This means that if you would have to decide about every little thing you do in the morning, by the time noon comes, you'd already be tired. I don't know about you, but I need that willpower for more important things later in the day. You don't want to be that person at a 3:00 p.m. meeting saying "Uhh... umm...I don't know...I can't decide." Gotta save that energy for things that matter.

Have you ever had that fuzzy, foggy feeling after you wake up where your brain feels like it's upside down? It has a name! It's called sleep inertia, and don't worry, it's normal, inevitable. almost. Studies have shown that regardless of sleep time and quality, it can last to up to two hours! In other words, don't go trying to fly a plane thirty minutes after you wake up... Okay, here is the good news: another study showed that behavioral modifications (a specific morning routine) helps reduce sleep inertia. For those of you with a very serious case of morning grogginess, here's the routine they used.

R   REFRAIN FROM SNOOZING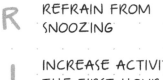

I   INCREASE ACTIVITY FOR THE FIRST HOUR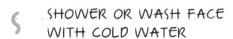

S   SHOWER OR WASH FACE WITH COLD WATER

E   EXPOSURE TO SUNLIGHT

U   UPBEAT MUSIC

P   PHONE A FRIEND

Last selling point, I promise. A morning routine could even improve your health. Mental, emotional, physical...the whole package! It can improve your sleep quality. After waking up at the same time for a few weeks, you'll notice you start to wake up naturally, which increases your energy levels during the day, and you'll start to get tired at an earlier, consistent time, which improves sleep quality at night. Health-inspired practices provide a space to get some mental clarity and take control of your life. The steadiness of a routine builds self-confidence and a sense of security and consistency that improves your emotional health. And, you know, if you decide to work out in the morning, or even have a healthier breakfast... yeah you guessed it, that helps your physical health, too!

So now do you see why you might *want* a morning routine? Yay! Let's create one, then...

A MORNING ROUTINE THAT FUELS PRODUCTIVITY

The idea is to create a routine that helps you transition from sleep mode into work mode. Once you start getting those small and, hopefully, inspiring tasks done, you'll start building *productive momentum*. In other words, once you start accomplishing tasks, you will transition into a productive mode and want to keep accomplishing other tasks. You might ask, what tasks? What should I include in my morning routine? Well... you have to start by asking yourself what kind of morning routine you would like. A relaxing one, an insightful one, an active one, a productive one, a little bit of everything? What is lacking in your day?

When I first asked myself, the answer was simple: productivity. Yeah, not that simple... So, I decided to figure out how I could create a morning ritual that would increase my productivity during the day. After following many versions of this kind of routine for many months, I became convinced that you can really morph any kind of morning routine into one that builds that productive momentum and inspires productivity if you just include some basic elements of productivity. This leaves us with the question: *What fuels productivity?*

I believe there are four key things without which your productivity will be seriously hindered.

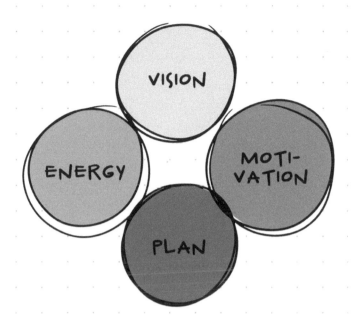

VISION: LOOK INTO THE CRYSTAL BALL

The definition of vision is the ability to think about or plan the future with imagination and wisdom. I love that definition because it encompasses something greater than just a plan on a piece of paper. Someone asks you: what's your vision? Your answer is not just a new position at your job, a new location for your house, a certain sum of money in your bank account, or a plan to achieve something. Your answer implicates why you want to achieve something, the way you want to feel when you have done so, and the person you want to become. You'll need a lot of imagination and wisdom for that.

Without a vision of where your life is going and what you want to achieve, you have no direction. How are you supposed to dedicate time and effort to something if there is no real purpose behind whatever you are doing? Having a clear vision means having a reason to wake up in the morning. Wouldn't you like to go to sleep at night with the satisfaction of knowing that at the end of the day, no matter how small your steps were, you moved forward? Or to go to sleep knowing that you'll have another chance to keep moving forward in just a few hours? How can you know you moved forward if you don't know where you are going? That is why having a clear vision is essential to your productive output. Does any of this sound familiar? A few chapters back, when we were talking about planning for our goals, the first thing we had to do was Time Travel and *visualize* our lives. Hold onto that vision not just for planning how to execute your goals, but for how you want to live every day of your life. The idea is to be reminded in even the slightest possible way of that vision during your morning routine.

ENERGY: REFUELING MAGIC

This seems like an obvious one, right? You need the physical energy to perform, there is just no way around that. We often focus on time management and learning to prioritize to make better use of our time, but that time is useless if we don't have the energy to complete our tasks. No breakfast? Gotta fill up that tank! It's not only important for your body and muscles, but for your brain, too; it also runs on food. Increasing your physical energy implies supplying your body with calories (eating) and getting it to produce chemicals that make you feel awake (exercising). Pretty simple, right? But what about your mental energy? Not your brain. Your mind. Feeding your mindset and motivation is crucial as well.

MOTIVATION: CHANNEL THE FORCE

You can have a purpose and all the energy in the world to do the things that you have to do, but what if you just don't want to…? "Ughhh where is my willpower? Why don't I have the discipline to just do things? Why can't I get myself to actually get up and go get it done?" Yep, that's pretty much all of us, at some point or another, and anyone who tells me differently… I don't buy it. In the end, you need that willingness to work out, read the book, study for three hours, cook that healthy meal, or actually focus on your work. Although sometimes, you have to simply power through and ignore your unwillingness to do something, creating that willingness sure seems a lot easier, and you can. Motivation will most likely be influenced by a million things, it can be internal and external, and it won't always be there, but the idea is to do *something* that motivates you to do the things you have to do.

PLAN: CRAFT IT ON PAPER

Surprised this one's part of productivity? This is a planning book, after all! All I have to say is this: you can't get much done without a good plan. I mean you can, just not as efficiently, in my humble opinion. And don't we all just love efficiency?

Okay, okay… I know what you're thinking: "That's all well and good, but *what* do I do?" Don't worry, I got you covered. Flip the page! But wait, before you do, answer this question: What would *you* like to do if you had one extra hour every morning?

MORNING ROUTINE IDEAS

VISION

- REVIEW YOUR GOALS
- REWRITE YOUR GOALS
- VISUALIZE YOUR GOALS
- SET A DAILY INTENTION
- PRACTCE GRATITUDE
- STATE YOUR PHILOSPHY
- JOURNALING
- MORNING PAGES
- VISION BOARD INSPO
- PRAY / READ SCRIPTURE
- MAKE YOUR OWN QUESTION OF THE DAY.
  EX: IF I WERE TO DO SOMETHING FOR MY FUTURE SELF TODAY, WHAT WOULD IT BE?

MOTIVATION

- DON'T HIT SNOOZE
- MAKE THE BED
- NO SOCIAL MEDIA
- JOURNAL
- WRITE AFFIRMATIONS
- GRATITUDE JOURNALING
- INSPIRATIONAL VIDEO
- LISTEN TO A PODCAST
- READ A DAILY QUOTE
- READ A BOOK
- SIT IN SILENCE
- STUDY SCRIPTURES
- LISTEN TO MUSIC
- TEXT/CALL A LOVED ONE

ENERGY

- WASH YOUR FACE
- DRINK A GLASS OF WATER (OR LEMON WATER)
- DRINK SOME COFFEE
- TAKE YOUR VITAMINS
- WAKE UP AT THE SAME TIME
- HANG OUT WITH YOUR FAMILY
- PLAY WITH YOUR PET
- ELEVATE YOUR HEART RATE
- RUN / WORKOUT / STRETCH / YOGA
- HAVE A HEALTHY BREAKFAST
- TAKE A FEW DEEP BREATHS
- LET THE SUNLIGHT IN
- MEDITATE
- JOURNAL
- SKIN CARE ROUTINE
- INCLUDE ANYTHING YOU ENJOY (YOUR FAVORITES)

PLAN

- REVIEW YOUR TO-DO LIST
- CALENDAR BLOCK
- MENTAL REVIEW OF YOUR DAY
- SET YOUR ONE BIG THING
- WORK ON YOUR SIDE HUSTLE
- WORK ON A PASSION PROJECT
- DO NOT CHECK EMAILS
- WEAR A UNIFORM
- PREP DAY'S MEALS

PICK AND CHOOSE

So, I decided to take all those things successful people do in the morning and group them into the four key elements of productivity, based on what they fuel. Of course, you may have different opinion on what category these fall under, and that's fine, do what works for you. The idea is to add at least *one of each* element to your morning routine, so you don't neglect any aspect of productivity.

You want to start your day by being reminded of what *your* **vision** is and what you want to get out of the next twenty-four hours. You could do this by rereading your goals, rewriting them, looking at your vision board, or any other way you can think of to be inspired to chase a future, better version of yourself. The important thing when choosing something to review your vision is that it grounds you, it makes you think about where you are right now and where you want to be, and most importantly, it urges you to start working for those goals.

When it comes to doing something in the morning to elevate your **energy** levels, there are a few basic things you can't go wrong with. Number one, eat a healthy breakfast. Pretty much speaks for itself. Number two, exercise. Getting your body active is underestimated by most of us. We tend to think that we are too busy or tired to work out (but not too busy for two forty-five-minute episodes of your favorite Netflix show), but it will increase your energy levels and make you feel happier—maybe not right away, give it a good two weeks and you should see a difference—and feel more productive. When you work out, your body increases the production of endorphins, chemicals that reduce the perception of pain and trigger a positive feeling in the body, similar to the effects of morphine. It's your personal painkiller/happiness/energy factory, and all you have to do is move! It increases your skin health by producing natural antioxidants and stimulating blood flow that delay aging! Should I keep going? It helps with relaxation and sleep quality; it can prevent chronic diseases like Type II diabetes and hypertension. It promotes flow of blood and oxygen to your brain, thus increasing its health. It improves your memory. I could go on and on about why you should exercise, but it will all be much easier if you just try it and get back to me.

All that being said, I hate that word. The very thought of exercising, going to the gym and doing something for the ultimate purpose of sweating... "Ughhhhh." I get it. It sucks. This is why I adopted a new policy towards exercise you may like. It all comes down to the mindset. The purpose behind me exercising is not to work out, but rather to *move* my body in whatever form I wish to that day, running for thirty minutes, walking, resistance or weight training, a fifteen-minute yoga practice, pilates, jumping up and down in the living room, lying down in the floor to stretch for five minutes. Just move. Most importantly, elevate your heart rate! If you start doing at least this, you'll see a huge change in your energy levels and your mental health.

Which leads me to number three, feed your mental energy. You can do this by meditating, journaling, breathing, and exercising. My preferred method for increasing my mental energy is by incorporating some of my "favorites" into my mornings. Having your favorite tea, eating your favorite breakfast, doing your favorite work out, lighting your favorite candles, and taking your sweet time to do all of these things creates a happy place right in the middle of your house. There is now a space for pleasure, tranquility, and balance in your life.

Motivation is the easiest. Pick something that motivates you, something external to you that makes you want to jump off the couch and get to work, something that inspires you to be the best version of yourself that day. That can be in the form of someone actually motivating you or something that simply has a positive influence on your mindset and mood. Internally, though, you have to build that motivation. This is where you can start building your productive momentum, by doing small tasks that will encourage you to do another task.

"I have to realize that I'm not in control of everything, but I am in control of some things, and I am in control of my reactions. I am in control to my responses to pressure."

—Janelle Monáe, singer, songwriter, and actress

Finally, **plan** for the day, for the week, for the month, etc. Decide how you will spend your energy that day. The planning aspect of productivity not only refers to actual time stamps and to-do lists, but also to prioritization. Plan to protect your morning routine by avoiding things that might interfere with your productivity, like checking your email, for example. Plan to make your mornings easier by eliminating choices; have the same breakfast every day or plan your outfit the night before. Plan to dedicate this special morning stamina and time to a side hustle you've been working on, or a project that inspires you, or a goal you're chasing after. This is *your* time. Prioritize yourself.

So, literally, pick and choose. Take a good long look at that list, pick the things that draw your attention and choose whether or not to make them a part of your routine. Of course, feel free to add any other things you might want to include; these are only some ideas to inspire you. Open your journal, create a Collection for "My Ideal Morning Routine," and write them down. We'll get to organizing and actually structuring your routine later. Trust me, just list those things you wish you could be doing on a regular basis on a piece of paper and bring them to life. You have nowhere to go but up. That blank page is filled with infinite possibilities, not just for the things you could do, but for the person you could become.

MY IDEAL MORNING BRAINDUMP

Dump all the things you wish you could include in your morning routine.
Don't worry about the order and logic, we'll deal with that later.

VISION

MOTIVATION

ENERGY

PLAN

NON-NEGOTIABLE MAGIC TOOLS

While I have been encouraging you to create your own morning routine and do what works for you, there are a few things that you might want to include in your routine to really boost your productivity. These are what I call my "Non-Negotiables." No matter how much my routine changes or how much time I have to rush somewhere in the morning, these are the four things that will always be a part of my ideal morning routine.

ONE ALARM

Oh, the snooze button, procrastination's best friend. It feels so satisfying to press that button and so irritating when the second alarm rings. We've all been slaves to the snooze button at some point in time, but once you get rid of this habit and get a taste of an irritation-free wake up routine, you will never be a victim of the snooze button again.

For starters, when you snooze your alarm, you go back to sleep for a very short period of time, hence a very short sleep cycle in which you will not reach a deep state of sleep. Therefore, you will wake up from this ineffective "nap" feeling groggy and sleepy, more so than if you had woken up the first time around. Studies show that snoozing your alarm increases sleep inertia by delaying physical activity and the psychological arousal associated with waking up. Most importantly, however, snoozing your alarm equals admitting defeat. You failed to accomplish the first task you set up for yourself—to wake up at the time your alarm rang. The first decision you made that day was to "not follow through," and you are sending a message of failure to your brain and reinforcing the opposite of productive momentum! No, no, no. Get up, wash your face, and be proud that you started the day with the right attitude to build your confidence. Stop snoozing your alarm and watch that ripple effect drastically change your day.

NO SHINY MANIPULATING BOX OF METAL

Your phone. Yep, it's manipulating you. That sounds very conspiracy theory-ish, and that is not at all what I mean. How long after you've opened your eyes do you check your phone? According to a 2017 survey in the United States, 62 percent of people check their phone within 15 minutes of waking up, 43 percent within 5 minutes, and 18 percent immediately.

Immediately.

You are not even vertical, and you're checking your phone!

Are you part of this club? I was for a very long time. We are so addicted to the endless thread of new information and instant un-lasting gratification that we haven't even had a glass of water before we've plunged into social media.

Honestly, think about it: why do you even check your phone? Novelty, ego boost, entertainment? To avoid something, maybe; boredom, responsibilities, hardships? Emergencies? Okay, fine...that last one's alright. And after you have checked your phone, what are you left with? Gratification, motivation, happiness? Did it change your plans? For the better or for the worse? Aside from dealing with any emergencies, if your job or family might need that from you, there is no real reason to check your phone right away.

Imagine this: Your alarm rings, and while still lying in bed, you grab your phone, and wake up to an unnatural blazing blue light piercing through the tiny space between your eyelids. You immediately open your Instagram account, only to be disappointed by the non-impressive gain in followers in your new account, despite considerable efforts to stay hooked on the comments section throughout the day. With an already dispirited mindset, you look at the rest of your notifications, only to be overwhelmed by the number of tiny little checkboxes to check, messages to answer, and tasks to accomplish. After a twenty-minute scroll spiral leading to stars' gossip, enviable pictures, and a sense of unescapable mundaneness, you decide to get up. "Great, now I'm late." So, you rush through your morning in an attempt to look presentable and get to wherever it is you have to be on time, and inevitably leave your morning to-do list with more than half of the tasks uncompleted and a subconscious lack in confidence to accomplish what you proposed to do that day.

That was me for way too long. It seems like a frivolous thing, checking your notifications, but it can so easily spiral into something much greater than that. If you have a healthy balance and manage to not get sucked into the world of negativity by checking your phone, by all means, do so; but if, in any way, your morning resembles that, please, just try not looking at your phone when you wake up...even for five minutes.

Focus on you before you tune into the rest of the world.

To clarify, it is not your phone that plays the villain here. If you use it in a productive, healthy way, keep at it. Just try to stay clear of social media and any work-related notifications. Focus on you before you tune into the rest of the world. If you must check your notifications for emergencies, give yourself at least five minutes before you do so, deal with them and then move on with your morning. The solution is quite simple. Don't leave your phone near your bed. That kills two bird with one stone as it will help you stop snoozing your alarm because you now have to get out of bed to turn it off. Block the apps that distract you. Use your journal for all planning, tracking, journaling, and logging you may be doing on your phone. Let the morning be yours, don't allow external influence until you are ready, and when you are, let those influences be positive ones.

QUIET INTROVERT TIME

This kind of relates to the "No Phone" policy. Find a time in the morning to stop and think, to acknowledge where you are in that moment, to be grateful for what you have, and to become aware of your thoughts and emotions. You can't have power over them or over your mindset if you can't recognize them. Find clarity. Find a time for you and your thoughts, whether you do this in the shower, while drinking your coffee, or while journaling. Whether it is for five minutes or thirty seconds, find that time for you and only you in the middle of a busy morning.

NO FRICTION

Similar to not wanting to be in a rush, you might not want your mornings to feel forced and unnatural. It takes time to get used to a routine, but it's in your best interest to make it as smooth as possible from the beginning. One action can take you to the next with the least amount of effort. We'll come back to this in a few pages, but, for now, keep in mind that you want it to be enjoyable.

CREATE YOUR IDEAL MORNING ROUTINE

You're not gonna go from waking up thirty minutes before work, snoozing the alarm three times, rushing to get ready, skipping breakfast, and any other disastrous way to start your day you can think of, to following a "perfect" morning routine from one day to the next. I wish we could, but that is neither realistic nor sustainable. Building habits, especially good habits, takes time. But that is okay because even by building one positive habit, your life will begin to change, and from that new-found confidence, you will start to build your way up into the morning you wish you could have. Today, we are going to create your ideal morning routine so you have something to aspire to, a version of you that you might want to chase after. So, forget about the technicalities for now, and let yourself dream big.

WHAT IS YOUR EARLIEST POSSIBLE WAKE UP TIME?

The length of your morning routine doesn't matter—you can still influence your day with a twenty-minute ritual. Taking into account your job or school, the travel time and the number of hours you wish to sleep, think about the earliest possible time you could wake up if you had your perfect morning routine. This will give you a time frame to work with.

WHAT MAKES IT TO YOUR LIST?

Forget about everyone else. Forget about what you are supposed to do. This is *your* time, you choose what you want to work on, what mood you want to be in, how you want to feel, what you want to dedicate your energy to, and how you want to boost your productivity. There are no rules, only suggestions. Here are some questions you could ask yourself that might help guide you to discover what will make it to your morning routine list.

WHAT ELSE MAKES IT TO YOUR LIST?

These questions can help you find other behaviors you might want to include in your ideal morning routine.

- WHAT DO YOU WANT TO DO IN YOUR MORNINGS?

- WHAT ARE YOUR VALUES AND HOW CAN YOU MANIFEST THEM IN THIS TIME?

- WHAT PROJECTS DO YOU WISH TO ACCOMPLISH?

- WHAT ARE YOUR PERSONAL GOALS? ARE THERE ANY BEHAVIORS YOU WANT TO ADD TO YOUR DAILY ROUTINES THAT MIGHT MAKE THOSE GOALS MORE ACHIEVABLE?

- WHAT COULD REALLY MOVE THE NEEDLE FOR YOU IN TERMS OF PRODUCTIVITY?

- WHAT ARE THE THINGS "PEOPLE" SAY YOU SHOULD DO IN THE MORNING THAT ACTUALLY INTEREST YOU?

- WHAT ARE THE NON-NEGOTIABLE THINGS THAT YOU HAVE TO INCLUDE IN YOUR MORNING ROUTINE?

Use your journal to go through this process so you can always look back at the things that interested you, and things that you might not be ready to start now, but might want to in the near future. Take a look at your Weekly Recaps and at your Monthly Review Sessions and find the things you've been meaning to start doing.

REVERSE ENGINEER YOUR MORNING

This is where you have to get a bit more realistic. Start taking into account your travel time and all the mundane things you have to do like brushing your teeth, showering, getting dressed, eating breakfast, etc. Consider how long some of your activities might take. Remember how we did this in the previous section? Start from the time you have to be somewhere and count back until you reach your wake-up time. Don't be stingy. Try to overestimate the amount of time a certain activity takes. You don't want to be late to school every day.

REVERSE ENGINEERING MY

MORNING ROUTINE

- leave for hospital — 6:10
- get ready/pack bags and lunch (20 min) — 5:50
- work on my book (1.15 hrs) — 4:45
- make tea/coffee + journaling (10 min) — 4:35
- get dressed + audiobook/podcast (15 min) — 4:20
- shower (10 min) — 4:10
- wake up + lemon water — 4:00

Context: This was my morning routine before going to the hospital during my intern year, while I was still writing this book.

TELL THE STORY

This might seem a bit of a weird step when it comes to making plans, but, in any scenario, if you want something to run very smoothly, this is a great way to detect the flaws in your plans. Once you have the final list of the things you want to include in your routine and you have reverse engineered the time it takes to do everything, try writing or at least telling a story of your morning. The idea is for you to start from the moment you wake up and narrate the things that you will do. Make sure to include the transitions from one thing to another, what room you are in, and when you are heading into the next room. This will help you identify the parts of your routine that don't make much sense and could create some friction in your mornings. For example, in my routine, I change into workout clothes as soon as I wake up and before I leave my bedroom. Even though I won't work out for another hour, when the time to work out does come, I don't want to have to walk back into my room and change. Writing down the steps and transitions will help you reorganize your routine so there is no friction at all.

Here are some other examples of my morning routines:

PACKED MORNINGS

- 5:50 • wake up + change for gym
- (E) 6:10 • gym / workout / yoga
- 7:00 • walk back home + rest / hangout
- 7:30 • shower
- (M) 7:45 • get ready + audiobook/podcast
- (E) 8:15 • breakfast
- (P) v 8:45 • journal (daily to-do list)
- (P) 9:00 • start studying

Context: This was my morning routine when I did not have to go to the hospital in the mornings and I incorporated working out in the morning to my routine.

LET'S GET TO WORK

6:30 • wake up & call Javi
(M) 6:45 • make the bed + skincare
(E) 7:00 • lemon water
(V) 7:10 • rewrite goals + read Daily Stoic
(M) 7:30 • get ready + audiobook/podcast
(P) (E) 8:00 • coffee + journal (daily to-do list)
(P) 8:15 • deep work
(E) 12:00 • breakfast

Context: This is my morning routine now, during quarantine
when I don't have anywhere to be in the mornings and a
big project to finish (writing this book).

START WITH ONE HABIT

Rome wasn't built in a day, and neither will your perfect
morning. Take it slow, start with *one* habit, maybe wake up only
five minutes before your current wake-up time, and work your
way up from there.

TRACK YOUR PROGRESS

We know by now that tracking your progress is a huge motivator to keep up with your good work. Create a "Habit Tracker" for the little habits you are trying to build with your morning routine and observe how you improve over time. Create a collection with your current morning routine so you can see how it changes over the years and how much you grow. Make your dot journal a part of your morning routine by creating spaces to journal, creating gratitude logs, and tracking the progress of the new habits you're building. Use it to document the results of having the productive morning routine. Write in your Daily Log how your day changed because of your morning routine.

Know that your routine will change and that you might try some things you hate doing or realize there are things you could be doing better or at another time. That is okay. Change is okay. So, don't be too rigid on yourself and try to enjoy this process. It is not this huge thing that you now have to do, but rather small things that, over time, will seem second-nature to you. There is no hurry, so be patient and enjoy your much-needed morning cup of coffee.

ALL THINGS DOT JOURNAL

So, at the end of my morning routine— or the beginning of my workday—I dive into my dot journal. This is always a part of my routine no matter how long or what the focus is. It's when I sit with my thoughts and maybe some music, and plan my day in the ways we talked about at the beginning of this book. This is when I practice the Morning Reflection I mentioned earlier. This is when I check off my habits, log anything I might be tracking, empty my brain, take a look at my goals, and scratch my dot journal like crazy. Remember that it's not just for planning, although that's a huge part of the morning ritual, right?

Use your dot journal to track every little thing you want and prioritize a few minutes in the morning to update your progress and to journal about what you're thinking or feeling and about the changes you want to see about who you want to be. Plan what you want to accomplish today. The morning is your sacred time to get your life together with ten minutes of journaling after you've primed your mind to be at its sharpest state. Now, go get it done.

Your Ideal

MORNING ROUTINE

START TIME:

END TIME:

TAKE IT TO THE NEXT LEVEL

Soon after starting a morning routine, you'll realize the real secret to a calm, inspiring morning routine lies in your evening routine. Let's make it magical, too.

CHAPTER 13

Planning for Some Downtime

Who doesn't want to have hours to relax and watch mindless TV? Maybe even have some cozy couch time with your family?

Let me tell you a secret.

Doing this will actually make you more productive. There! Now you have the perfect excuse to sit on the couch and relax, because, trust me, it'll work. Okay, okay, I know I'm not making much sense...let me explain.

WHY YOU NEED AN EVENING ROUTINE

Prioritizing rest and relaxation in a healthy and fulfilling way will eventually lead to a happier, more wholesome life. You won't be as tired during the day because you will have provided your body the rest it so desperately needs. Because you have a designated time to relax and indulge in your cravings, you are less likely to be looking for ways to satisfy them during the day. If you know that you get to enjoy yourself at night, you won't have the need to constantly try to "enjoy" bits and pieces of your day that really just distract you from your work.

An evening routine will bring closure to your day and inspire that feeling of a "fresh start" the following day. Once you get in the habit of disconnecting from your busy life, you will wake up feeling recharged enough to go do the things you have to get done. Taking the time to pause and reflect upon your day, to rest and to go to sleep with a clear mind, will make tomorrow much easier. Even better than that, it will make your mornings easier. This is where you get ready for your morning routine and where you look forward to what you get to do the next day and where you prepare for whatever your calendar looks like. More importantly, however, it is your sacred space for pause. All day, we're moving at one hundred miles per hour without ever stopping to realize how it is we're feeling, without taking a real break, without really unplugging from everything that is external to us. In this time, you are *free* to disconnect. It's okay. More than okay, it's exactly what you need.

FROM HECTIC TO GROUNDED

Do you know the difference between the pause and the stop button (back when we used DVD players to watch movies)? Well, the pause button will freeze the film until you hit the button again, allowing you to continue where you left off. If you hit the stop button, however, the film is interrupted. Stopping ends the film.

When it comes to your life, your job, your responsibilities...are you pausing? Or stopping? Are you momentarily taking a break, resting, yet remaining ready to start right where you left off, or are you completely disconnecting, so much that it feels like you have to start all over the next day? Are you draining yourself by watching *too many* hours of mindless TV? Are you waking up too tired because you went to sleep too late? Are you making it harder for yourself to get up and do what you are supposed to because you dissociated from your responsible self? Are you pausing? Or stopping?

Don't get me wrong, detaching completely is great every once in a while, but not on a regular basis. Doing so only increases that friction you feel when you wake up, the sleepiness, the discontent, and the unnecessary, added effort to actually wake up. No. We need to pause. We want to create an evening routine that is grounding. One where we can realize where we stand at that moment. How am I feeling? How much did I achieve today? Am I proud of this? What can I do better tomorrow? What am I grateful for today? You need a breathing space, a moment where you can look back on your day, acknowledge where you are, and decide how to move forward.

WIND DOWN CHECKLIST

Because the evening starts at a different time for everyone, there is much less structure to build on when it comes to creating your ideal evening routine. For some people, the evening starts the moment they get off work, around 5:00 p.m., leaving them with plenty of time to get stuff done and slowly start to wind down. All through med school, my evening routine began around 9:00 p.m. after my last class of the day. In cases like mine, your evening routine might be more of a "let's prep for bed ASAP" kind of routine. That's fine. Again, do whatever works for you. Much like with our morning routine, there is no perfect recipe, but rather a combination of practices you can do, with intention, to get the results you want. Regardless of the amount of time or the focus of your evening routine, in the end, you want to close our day in a positive healthy way. Inspired. Ready. Grounded.

There are four key steps to include in an evening routine. What we're aiming for, really, is a process that allows us to transition from the boisterous day we've had by reflecting on it into the next day, by preparing for it, relaxing, and getting the rest we need.

REFLECT

Take a few minutes to look back on your day and analyze. You can use this time to think about the things that have the most impact on your life.

This can be done through the Reflections we talked about at the beginning of the book. In Carroll's method, this would be the p.m. Reflection. He suggests that at the end of the day, you should look at your tasks, notes, and events, and reflect upon each one, especially the ones you haven't done yet, and decide if they are worth your time. If they're not, are they something you can delegate, or something you can just eliminate? If they are, how important or urgent are they? When are you going to make the time to get them done? The Bullet Journal Method, like a planner, allows for this thought process to be a conscious one, because you have to manually "migrate" or cross out a task. Don't skip this process. It's important. It will make you feel in control of your day and your life. It will allow you to be proactive and plan ahead with purpose. Only by knowing where you stand will you know how to move forward.

Most people already do this at the end of their "work" day, but I'm encouraging you to go deeper and to do it consciously. Don't just look at your pending to-dos. Look at your accomplishments, your mood, and anything you think is worth highlighting. Check off your habits, log anything you might be tracking, reflect on your Daily Log, practice some gratitude, and maybe even plan a little bit of tomorrow. Use your journal to close your day.

PREPARE

 Set everything up for the next day, and I mean *everything*. Tidy up your desk space, charge your devices, lay out the clothes for the next day, pack your lunch, wash the remaining dirty dishes, ready your bag... everything. Just set up everything that you can, especially if you know it will make your morning easier. It sounds like a lot of work, but honestly, it takes a lot less than you expect, and even less than that if you make a habit out of it!

Set everything back to neutral. There is no better feeling than waking up to a neutral space. Your day suddenly feels like it's January 1st and full of possibility. At least for me, I'm kind of obsessed with clean slates and the 1st of whatever, as you can see. What I really mean by setting your space back to neutral is to put everything back where it belongs, back to a state where it is ready to be used again, without the crumbs of the day before or the reminders of your failed attempts to focus. A nice, clean, neutral state.

> **NOUN** A CULINARY PROCESS IN WHICH INGREDIENTS ARE PREPARED AND ORGANIZED BEFORE COOKING.

In my evening routine, this habit is called "**mise-en-place**." This is a concept I first learned from my stepfather. (He's a chef. My favorite chef, in fact, and I'm not at all biased.) Whenever we were going to cook something together, he would ask us or help us to set everything up. On one of our cooking adventures, he said to me, "Do the mise-en-place and I'll be right there," turned around, and left. "The what!?" I'm sure he had explained this concept to me before, because that's who he is, but in the moment, I had no idea what he was talking about. Naturally, I googled it. Terribly misspelled, of course. I did an awful job of setting everything up to cook our new-found chili recipe, and I remember him helping me gather everything that we needed, setting it all up on the counter, and teaching me about the concept again with all of the patience in the world. I didn't really "use" the concept until I started building the habit of setting everything up. One night, I realized: "This is just like what my father does with the ingredients for his recipe. I'm going to place them exactly where I'll need them tomorrow." That's when I renamed the habit in my tracker from "pick up" to "mise-en-place." So much more inspiring. You're welcome to steal that idea, if you want.

Make a list in your journal of the things you need to prepare for the next day and use it as a reference every night. Sooner rather than later, you won't need the list anymore.

MISE-EN-PLACE
✓   10 MINUTE TIDY
✓   DESKTOP BACK TO NEUTRAL
✓   CLEAN KITCHEN
✓   LAY OUT TOMORROW'S CLOTHES

RELAX

Now, this is where you get to indulge. Do whatever you want... sort of. Just do something that you believe to be relaxing, maybe something that is not productive or perfect or the healthiest possible thing you could be doing at the moment. Find a time where you can escape your to-dos and spoil yourself. You've earned it. You're ready for the next day. You've reflected and hopefully planned a little, you've set everything up, now you get to rest. Guilt free. Watch some TV, scroll on social media, have some leisure time with your family, do nothing, if that's what you want. This is your time to waste, or better yet, to enjoy wasting, because you need this. Your body, your brain and your willpower need to pause and relax, to disconnect, for just a little while.

SLEEP

 So, I don't just mean sleep. Of course, sleeping seven to nine hours is extremely important and will make or break your productivity the following day, but there is more to sleep than that. It's not just about the quantity of sleep, but also the *quality* of sleep. Yes! Sleep can be improved or worsened, of course, and it all comes down to your habits. This combination of habits is something doctors call "Sleep Hygiene." They are all scientifically proven habits that will increase your sleep quality. In fact, this is the first treatment option for insomnia. Doctors usually give these habits a chance before they turn to pharmaceuticals for treatment.

Of course, you might not have to implement all of these, but take a look at the list and think about the things you could be doing a bit better to improve your sleep quality. Try to include some of those in your routine. My suggestion is that at least thirty minutes before your ideal bedtime, you focus solely on going to sleep in the best, healthiest way possible.

SLEEP HYGIENE

- Regular sleep and wake times
- Avoid naps
- Refrain from stimulating activities too close to bedtime
- Avoid caffeine preferably past lunch
- Only be in bed to sleep, refrain from laying in it during the day
- If you can't fall asleep, get out of bed and do something relaxing and then come back to bed when you're tired
- Don't eat too close to bedtime
- Avoid nicotine or alcohol in the evening
- Refrain from electronics or any form of blue light before bed
- Set up your bedroom to be cool, dark and quiet

EVENING ROUTINE IDEAS

REFLECT

- GO THROUGH YOUR TO-DO LIST
- MIGRATE UNFINISHED TASKS
- FILL IN YOUR HABIT TRACKER
- PRACTICE GRATITUDE
- LONG-FORM JOURNALING
- TODAY'S WINS
- PRAY / READ SCRIPTURE
- MAKE YOUR OWN QUESTION OF THE DAY.
  EX: HOW DID I GROW TODAY?

PREPARE

- MISE-EN-PLACE
- PLAN TOMORROW'S OUTFIT
- LEAVE GYM CLOTHES OUTSIDE
- PACK LUNCH
- PREPARE MEALS FOR TOMORROW
- TIDY THE HOUSE
- CLEAN KITCHEN
- CREATE TOMORROW'S TO-DO LIST
- DECIDE TOMORROW'S SCHEDULE

RELAX

- GET OFF SOCIAL MEDIA
- SPEND TIME WITH FAMILY
- COOK DINNER
- READ A BOOK
- WATCH AN EPISODE OF YOUR FAVORITE TV SHOW
- CALL A LOVED ONE
- TAKE A SHOWER / BATH
- JOURNAL
- MEDITATE
- YOGA / WORKOUT
- PLAY GAMES

SLEEP

- HAVE A SET BEDTIME
- DIM THE LIGHTS AFTER SUNSET (OR ONLY USE YELLOW LIGHT)
- BE IN BED, WITHOUT YOUR PHONE AT LEAST 15-30 MINUTES BEFORE YOU HAVE TO BE ASLEEP
- NO ELECTRONICS IN THE BEDROOM
- SET UP A LAVENDER DIFUSER
- READ BEFORE / IN BED
- JOURNAL BEFORE / IN BED
- DRINK SOME BEDTIME TEA
- SKINCARE BEFORE BED

MY TIPS FOR A STRESS-FREE SHUTDOWN

There are a few things to keep in mind when it comes to creating a perfect evening ritual.

SYMBOLIC START

Try to pick something that will flip the switch in your brain from busy, noisy, productive life to whatever your evening routine's intention is. There has to be an activity that not necessarily starts your routine but transitions your mood and mindset. An alarm is not enough. For some people, that can be leaving work or walking into their homes, for others, walking out of their home office, working out, changing into cozy clothes, or maybe eating dinner.

My symbolic start is a shower—a hot, pampering shower. Now, it's not the first thing on my evening routine, but that's fine because this is the point in my ritual where I want to transition my mood and my mindset to "let's rest and get ready for bed." So, pick something that breaks up your day and allows you to move into your evening routine seamlessly.

DIMMED LIGHTS AND A CANDLE

Oh, and a cup of tea, hopefully. Set the mood. Your surroundings matter. They make a difference, whether you are aware of it or not. Do something that accompanies that relaxed mood you're craving.

WILL DO VS. COULD DO

Because part of the goal of this evening routine is to relax, you might not want to be too rigid when planning for it. This is why I encourage you to clearly signify the things that you must do as a part of your routine from the things that you could do. This way you won't feel like there are ten habits that you need to stick to every night, but rather only a few key habits and many other suggestions for a good night's rest. I also recommend that those key habits are the only ones you track; no need to add extra pressure to yourself. The point is to indulge and be free of obligations for little while.

You can create a journal spread of little things that bring you joy that you can refer to when you have some extra time in the evenings.

FOR THE NIGHT OWLS

I know that for you, a routine that is basically preparing for bed seems like a waste of potential productive time. While you might be going to bed later than most of us, you still need a healthy sleep routine, and you still need pause and rest. You might be choosing to work during those dark hours, unlike us early birds, and that's fine. Incorporate that into your routine and make its intention **"Quiet Productivity"** or something along those lines. Maybe even include some aspects of the morning routine to build your productivity if you need to, but once you are done being productive, make sure to prioritize rest and sleep hygiene. Make sure you still reflect upon your day and prepare your space and relax and hopefully, sleep the number of hours your body needs. I'm not encouraging you to fight your nature, but rather to work with it in a healthy way. Pick the bits and pieces that work for you and that make you feel proud and inspired the following day.

NOUN A STATE OF BEING PRODUC-TIVE IN AN UNINTERRUPTED FOCUSED MANNER.

Evening Routine For
NIGHT OWLS

START TIME: 6:00 PM

GAIN PRODUCTIVE MOMENTUM
6:00 • WORKOUT
7:00 • SHOWER + COOK DINNER
8:00 • SHORT EVENING TO-DO LIST
8:10 • PRODUCTIVE HOURS

SHUT DOWN (BEDTIME ROUTINE)
REFLECT:
11:00 • JOURNAL TOMORROW'S TO-DO LIST

PREPARE:
11:15 • MISE-EN-PLACE, DIM THE LIGHTS

RELAX:
11:30 • FREE TIME

SLEEP:
12:15 • GET READY FOR BED, NO MORE
ELECTRONICS, LIGHTS OUT

BED TIME: 12:30 AM

CREATE AN EVENING ROUTINE

The process for creating an evening routine is very similar to creating a morning routine: set a time frame to work with, decide what things you might want to do, reverse engineer from your bed time to your start time, and rearrange to reduce the friction. Use your journal to create a tracker like we did with the morning routine so you can see your progress. Use it to spend some quiet time meditating on your day and preparing for the next one. By taking a few minutes to reflect and journal about your day, your progress, and your wins, you make sure to pause for the evening, instead of stopping. Here are some of my evening routines:

SLOWLY WIND DOWN

- Ⓡ 5:30 • shutdown (to-do list + plan)
- Ⓢ 6:00 • workout
- Ⓡ 6:45 • free scroll time + dim lights
- Ⓟ 7:15 • 10 minute tidy / mise-en-place
- Ⓢ 7:30 • shower + pjs
- 8:00 • cook dinner
- Ⓡ 8:30 • tv time / free time
- Ⓢ 9:45 • go to bedroom + read

Context: This is my evening routine now, during quarantine, where I don't have classes so I have a lot of time to make the most out of the evening

GET TO BED ASAP

- Ⓡ 9:00 • relax + dinner + chat with Javi
- Ⓡ 10:00 • evening review + plan tomorrow
- Ⓟ 10:15 • mise-en-place
- Ⓟ 10:25 • pick tomorrow's outfit
- Ⓢ 10:30 • get ready for bed, dim lights
- Ⓢ 10:45 • in bed read/journal

Context: This is my evening routine when I had classes in med school. Usually I would get home around 9 pm so the goal was to go to sleep ASAP.

Now it's time to create your own.

MY IDEAL EVENING BRAINDUMP

Dump all the things you wish you could include in your evening routine.
Don't worry about the order or logic you'll create the final draft on the next spread

 REFLECT

 PREPARE

 RELAX

 SLEEP

Your Ideal
EVENING
ROUTINE

START TIME:

- ○
- ○
- ○
- ○
- ○
- ○
- ○
- ○
- ○
- ○

BED TIME:

CHAPTER 14

Sunday Is Your New Favorite Day

In order to bring in that clean slate feeling into my life on a regular basis, I practice a weekly reset routine, more specifically, my Sunday Reset. We talked about clean slates when I explained the Weekly Check-In. Well, the Sunday Reset is a set of small tasks to-dos that will help you run down the previous week and prepare you for the next one. It includes the Weekly Check-In. The idea is to find a moment of pause to slow down, look back at the days that have passed, and ensure that you'll stay on top of everything the following week. By constantly taking the time to tidy your space up, go through your journal, and strategize your future, you'll create a fresh start at the beginning of each week. With that comes a fresh doze of motivation and energy to tackle the things you said you were going to do and set clear deadlines for them as well.

THE ESSENTIALS

There are four things I like to take care of every week in order to stay productive and get my life together.

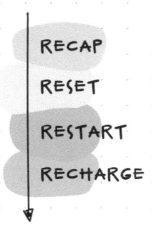

Recap: review the previous week.

Reset: clean up your spaces.

Restart: prepare for the week ahead.

Recharge: give your body and soul the rest it deserves.

If you can do at least one thing in each of those categories, I guarantee you'll feel refreshed and ready for Monday. The goal is to find some way to recap, reset, restart, and recharge on a regular basis. What you do, however, is not set in stone. Throughout this chapter, I'll be sharing examples of my own routine as well as other ideas. Feel free to pick and choose what works for you.

When I started to create my routine a few years ago, I was eager to do everything in my power to have the perfect week. I crammed my routines with twenty tasks, too many hours of meal prepping, and an excessively tiring cleaning routine. This, in turn, defeated the purpose of the routine itself: to make me feel energized for the week ahead.

I don't like having a to-do list on Sunday. It's my break day where I don't have to be responsible or abide by any lists or rules, and yet, I love my Sunday Routine. The reason for that is that I limit the things I do. I've pared them down to the tasks that have the most impact. I spend, at most, one hour of actually sitting down at my desk, going through my checklist. The rest of my routine, I do throughout the day, whenever I feel like it. Make sure that your routine is not overwhelming.

In order to boil down your routine to the essentials, find the things that would have the most impact in *your* life. Remember, you don't want your weekend to be a workday, you just want to do enough to give you a sense of control over the following week. For example, I know that having a messy space will diminish my productivity because I will inevitably tidy before I start working, therefore, I try to clean up on Sundays so that my space is ready on Monday. The same goes for having a clear game plan. It's impossible for me to start working if I don't have an outline of what I want to accomplish during the week. To avoid wasting time during my work week, I plan on Sunday so I'm ready to go Monday morning. Find what causes friction in your life and try to tackle it during the weekend.

LET'S BRAINDUMP

WHAT'S GETTING IN THE WAY
OF YOUR PRODUCTIVITY?

WHAT DAILY TASKS STRESS YOU OUT?

WHAT THINGS WEIGH YOU DOWN THE MOST?

WHAT THINGS CAN BE MADE EASIER BY
TACKLING THEM DURING THE WEEKEND?

RECAP

REVIEW THE PREVIOUS WEEK	IDEAS
• FILL IN HABIT TRACKER	• BRAINDUMP OPEN-LOOPS
• WEEKLY REFLECTION	• JOURNAL ON YOUR WEEK
• GO THROUGH TASKS INBOX	• MOST VALUABLE LESSONS
• GO THROUGH BRAINDUMP LIST	• REVIEW GOAL PROGRESS
• SORT BULLET JOURNAL	• BUDGET/FINANCE CHECK IN
• SORT IMPORTANT NOTES	• FAVORITE MEMORIES
• CURATE SOMETIME SOON LIST	• FILE TO-DOS, NOTES, IDEAS

You've spent a whole week writing entries in your journal, capturing your ideas, working on your habits, getting things done, and now it's time to take all that experience and polish it. This is when you review the previous week. The idea is to look at what you captured during the week—ideas, notes, pending tasks, memories, lists, everything—and sort it out. As David Allan would say, go through your various "inboxes." As you review the information you've captured, relocate it where it belongs.

This is especially powerful in your journal. If you've allowed your notebook to serve as a catchall for everything that goes through your mind, chances are, the last few pages are messy and filled with ideas and information that you might need to reference in the future. At the end of each week, flip through the last few pages and find what needs to be filed properly. Maybe you wrote down something you need to purchase. Transfer it to your "To Buy" list. Maybe you wrote down a goal you'll want to pursue in the future. Migrate it to your "Future Goals List." Any ideas that you might have captured, transfer them to a list you'll reference when looking for that idea.

For example, I have a dedicated page in my journal for ideas for Plan For Productivity. This week, I came up with a way to organize the main page in my website. Of course, I was busy all week, so I just wrote it down on my Daily Log for that day, and at the end of the week, as I flipped through these pages, I found my idea and transferred it to the "PFP Ideas" spread. This way, when I decide to dedicate some time to my website, I know where to look for ideas and I can find all the ones I've come up with so far. On the other hand, if I have some time the following week, instead of transferring it to the "PFP Ideas" spread, I might have added it as a to-do on next week's spread.

This natural flow of ideas is powerful. It allows you to dedicate time to them on your terms, yet keep them alive in your journal. The same concept applies to any piece of information. If you wrote it down in your Daily Logs, migrate it to where it belongs. For all the mini-projects you might have come up with, write them in your Sometime Soon List. Everything that you capture should have a place to go, one that's easy to reference when you need it.

Magic Trick: To avoid rewriting pieces of information, use the reference symbol we talked about earlier. Mine is: ▷

In whatever list I'm migrating my task to, I'll write the title followed by the symbol and the page number where the rest of the information is located, so I know where to look for it.

Most of us however don't have a productivity system based solely on the dotted journal. We have apps, note taking systems, task managers, project managers, email, calendars, mail, etc. This is the perfect time to go through the ones you use the most to make sure they stay up-to-date. Apply the same concept. Find what to keep, what to eliminate, and what to move into next week's task list. In the beginning, this may sound daunting, but if you do this on a regular basis, you'll realize these inbox are not overflowing with tasks and you'll be able to go through them fairly quickly.

Finally, once you've sorted all of your information, go through your Weekly Reflection. Ask yourself the questions that will allow you to close out your week and help you figure out how to navigate through the next one.

MY RECAP

- NOTES, TASKS, GOOGLE KEEP INBOX
- FILL IN ALL MY LOGS/TRACKERS
- WEEKLY REFLECTION
- BRAINDUMP OPEN-LOOPS
- SORT MY BULLET JOURNAL

The recap is about doing something valuable with your information and your experiences. It's about finding what's worth keeping. It's about recapping your life so you know where you stand, and therefore, how to move forward. Now it's time to create yours:

RECAP

Take some time to brain storm what you can do on your reset.

What things can you do that would help you learn and gather the most information from the past week?

1

2

3

RESET

CLEAN UP YOUR SPACES	IDEAS
• FRESH SHEETS & TOWELS	• CLEAR EMAIL INBOX
• TIDY UP YOUR HOUSE	• CLEAR DOWNLOADS
• PLAN TO USE UP LEFT OVERS	• CLEAR DESKTOP
• EMPTY ALL TRASHCANS	• REORGANIZE FILES
• TIDY YOUR WORKSPACE	• EMPTY COMPUTER TRASH
• GO THROUGH MAIL	• SPACES BACK TO NEUTRAL
• LOAD OF LAUNDRY	• CURATE LAST WEEK'S PHOTOS

Your environment has a huge impact on your mood, productivity, and motivation. We are visual creatures and our surroundings affect us. The color, the symmetry, the aesthetic, the temperature, the light, the smells, the clutter, the balance, it all influences you whether you're acutely aware of it, like me, or not. So, if your surroundings are almost always in your control, why not make them work for you instead of against you?

This is crucial. This is the part of the Sunday Reset that ensures I get a clean slate feeling. To me, resetting is about cleaning up my spaces. Yes, plural. It's not just about cleaning your house, in fact, that's the one I do the least of. It's about setting all of your spaces back to neutral including your physical space, your digital space, your workspace, and whatever other space you currently need refreshed.

Of course, cleaning is the way to go. There is just something so satisfying about a clean space, not to mention the small dose of pride and motivation that comes with having cleaned it yourself. But, wait. Do not get me wrong. I hate cleaning. I love clean spaces but hate the process. So, I'll be the first to tell you that you do not have to spend all of your Sunday sanitizing every hidden corner of your house. I mean, unless that's your kind of thing. I simply clean the spaces I use the most and make sure that everything is *tidy*. This means having clear countertops, no mess on the living room, neat couch cushions, no dishes in the sink, and having a clutter-free space. It's okay that you don't want to spend your day off mopping your life away. Find the routine that works for you.

While your house is probably the most significant, your digital and work spaces need refreshing as well. There is something about a messy desktop that just makes me cringe. All those files, no order, no structure, all the icons splattered over your best friend's face on the wallpaper...it's a nightmare. Our brain perceives clear and empty spaces as freedom to be filled with anything we might come up with. Also, having a "tidy" computer favors a smoother workflow. It saves you time and energy and allows you to stay up-to-date. I normally save *everything* to my desktop. So, I always clear my desktop, downloads, trash, and inbox at the end of the week. This way, I keep my files organized since I can move them to their appropriate folder. This quick routine guarantees I have a sparkling computer, ready for work.

MY RESET

- FRESH SHEETS & TOWELS
- TIDY KITCHEN, LIVING ROOM, BEDROOM
- EMPTY ALL TRASHCANS
- CLEAR EMAIL INBOX
- CLEAR DOWNLOADS, DESKTOP, TRASH

There is so much power in resetting your spaces. It leads to mental clarity. Understand and appreciate the fact that outer order breeds inner calm, as Gretchen Rubin says. Create the ideal space for your ideas to flow, your brain to be focused, and your mind to be calm. By setting your space back to neutral, you're fabricating a clean fresh start where everything is possible. More importantly, you just proved to yourself that you can pull your life together. This makes it more likely you'll follow through the next week. What would you like to reset on a regular basis?

RESET

Take some time to brain storm what you can do on your reset:

What things can you do that will help you go into the week feeling fresh and with a clean slate?

1

2

3

RESTART

PREPARE FOR THE WEEK AHEAD	IDEAS
• NEXT WEEK'S BUDGET	• WORKOUTS FOR THE WEEK
• WEEKLY SPREAD/BOARD	• UPDATE NEXT WEEK'S TASK LIST
• MEAL PLAN	• CALENDAR BLOCK
• MEAL PREP	• UPDATE EVENTS
• WEEK'S OUTFITS	• PLAN A FUN ACTIVITY
• REVISIT GOALS	• SET THE INTENTION FOR THE WEEK
• PLAN AHEAD FOR PROJECTS	• DEFINE WEEKLY MILESTONES

While resetting ensures that clean slate feeling, restarting ensures that you feel equipped to make the most out of that fresh start. It's all about preparing yourself for the week ahead. Yes, this means making plans! It's my favorite part, of course.

Remember all the way back in Part I when we talked about the Weekly Board? Well, this is where you get it done. We've already gone through our review in the recap portion of Sunday, and now it's time to use that information and plan the following week. In other words, create the Weekly Board to include the areas of your life you might need present this week. For example, you might have events coming up, tasks that need to get done, meals you plan to cook, and most importantly, your plan for how you'll work on your goals this week.

Take this time to go through the goals you're working towards and ask yourself what you can do this week in order to move forward. Revisit your projects, your milestone map, and your goals list for the month, and include that in the "Goals" section of your Weekly Board. This way, you make sure that you stay on track with your goals. I take this time to calendar block some events and big tasks, update my projects, plan for my goals, and create the Weekly Board.

MY RESTART

- MEAL PLAN
- UPDATE TASKS, GOALS, PROJECTS
- FINANCE UPDATE
- WEEKLY BOARD + CALENDAR BLOCK

During this time, the idea is to plan for anything that needs planning this week. Sometimes that means checking in with the people who might help you, and this is a good time to do so. Other times, that means setting up alarms so you don't forget what you need to do or where you need to be. And, at times, it might mean prepping meals for the entire week since you'll be too busy to cook. What you do during the reset changes, and that's fine. Find the things you can do that'll save you time or energy in the upcoming week. What matters is that you are doing *something* that makes you feel ready for the week ahead. Devise your game plan.

RESTART

Take some time to brain storm what you can do on your reset:

What things can you do to be best prepared for the upcoming week?

1

2

3

RECHARGE

REST | IDEAS

- ENJOY FAMILY TIME
- WATCH A MOVIE
- CALL A FRIEND/FAMILY
- SKINCARE
- READ A BOOK

- NATURE WALK
- ENJOY A NICE BRUNCH
- INDULGE
- DO WHATEVER YOU ENJOY
- DO NOTHING

Okay, I take it back, *this* is my favorite part of the Sunday Reset. This is all about you. Well, you and the people you love... sometimes. Take this little piece of your week to do whatever recharges your energy. This will change depending on who you are and what you need. What I do might not sound peaceful or appealing to you, so I'm just going to skip that. I do want to say that you should try to make these things as positive as you can. Try not to force yourself to do something you don't feel like doing. You have the rest of the week for that. Pamper yourself. Think about things that might actually have an impact on your life, your mood, and your overall happiness. Do more of the things that feed your energy and leave you feeling recharged.

MY RECHARGE

- CALL FAMILY
- PAMPERING SHOWER
- SKINCARE

If you prefer, you can change it up every week. In my experience, however, sticking to a few core activities that you love and incorporating them into a weekly routine is so much more powerful. It creates a sense of security, knowing that no matter how hard your week is, you'll always have that calm space for you to turn to during the weekend. This is the time to make yourself, your mental health, and your small doses of happiness your number one priority. We all need some self-care, and you can have it guilt-free. Embrace the little things that bring you joy.

RECHARGE

Take some time to brain storm what you can do on your reset:

What things can you do to rest and go into the following week with energy and contentment?

1

2

3

CREATING YOUR SUNDAY RESET

This routine is much less structured than the previous ones. I suggest you take a good look at the brain-dumps you made and try to pare them down even further to the things that will serve you the most. Having a fancy checklist with a million things to go through on Sunday will probably stress you out more than relax you. Instead, keep it as small as possible, so you can enjoy your weekend and still get a fresh start for Monday.

My policy is to have the list of the things I'd like to get done even though I won't get to all of them. Some weeks, I might not meal prep at all, others I don't clean my computer. It's okay. The idea is to have a safe ritual that recharges your energy for the upcoming week and that allows you to keep your life together.

LET'S BE REAL

Your routine will be unique and tailored specifically to you. If you have kids, you'll most likely want to spend the day with them, not cleaning your house. If you have to work on Sundays, then maybe Sunday isn't the best day to this reset; pick a day that works for you. Sunday is just my favorite day. Regardless of what your life looks like, find the space to pause. Light a candle and think. Reflect. Plan. Use your journal. This is how you build the puzzle of your life; this is where you connect the dots. Everything in life needs upkeep, so do your plans, and so do you. Make sure you're making that a priority. Stay on top of your life by checking in once a week. I can guarantee that this is a good investment of your time, and it'll only take one week of doing this routine for you to prove me right. Reset on Sunday and seize the week.

my **sunday reset**

RECAP

RESET

RESTART

RECHARGE

CHAPTER 15

Connecting the Dots : Keep the Magic Going

Why am I so obsessed with routines? Well, they just make life easier. They take all the decision-making out of a process and give you a set of instructions on what you need to do in order to accomplish a goal. The morning routine, evening routine, and even the Sunday routine are bonuses. You can live without them. But your planning routine is crucial—if you want to keep your life together, at least. The great thing about it is that you don't actually have to create a routine for it! As long as you sit down for ten minutes to take control of your life through planning, you're doing it. Get in the habit of sitting down with your journal and strategizing about your life with love and compassion. No pressure. No task list to follow. No judgement.

In this chapter, I'll walk you through the different moments in time when you can go through a mini planning routine. Unlike the rest of the book, however, I urge you—instead of making a list of things to do during that routine—to explore what comes naturally to you. Your planning routine should not be overly structured and demanding. Instead, keep it light and enjoyable. Find the things that will make your life easier in the future. Pick the bits and pieces of these routines that you know will benefit you, and experiment with them. Let me know if your life changes.

PREVIEW THE YEAR

Once a year, aside from planning for your yearly goals, it's important to scheme a little bit about how you want the year to look. Your Future Log is great tool for that. This is a dynamic spread that you'll be adding to throughout the year which will help you bring awareness to the things that are coming up. Use it as a reference when you're planning the little details behind each of these commitments in your other planning routines.

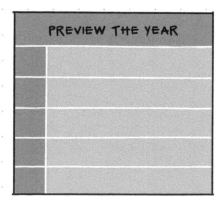

OUTLINE THE MONTH

Alright, we've got events scheduled throughout our year and some of the goals we'd like to accomplish in however many days are left of the year. It's time to plan for them in our monthly planning session. As I mentioned before, I like to have these big life-sorting sessions at the end of every month because that's enough time to have given any goals and habits a try, accomplished milestones, tackled projects, and actually seen some progress.

This monthly planning session is the perfect time to click into proactive mode. It's where you create a strategy to get "ahead of the puck, instead of chasing after it," as Lewis Howes said in his podcast episode *How to Win*. The basic principle, in order to achieve this, is to have a clear glance at what your commitments for the next month are.

Before planning anything, however, we need to review our previous month. This is the perfect time to take a look at your goals and reflect on your progress. Figure out where you're currently at and how you want to move forward.

So, what can you strategize for in these monthly planning sessions? I plan for three basic things every month: my commitments, my goals, and those goals' actions. This is where you look at your Future Log and migrate anything scheduled for the upcoming month to your Monthly Log. Keep it as minimal as possible. The idea is to figure out what you need to be prepared for and plan for it accordingly.

Once you've handled your previous commitments, you can strategize for goals you set up for this month. This is where you go into the details about how you're going to make them happen. Jot down notes, strategies, ideas, or habits you might want to build. Don't leave anything out. Look back at your Milestone Map and come up with a Battle Blueprint for the month's goals. Air Your Ambitions. Just as an FYI, I'm usually only working on one long-term project at a time. This makes it easy to squeeze it into my calendar and prioritize what truly matters.

Finally, and probably most importantly, this session is when you create the trackers that will keep you accountable—habit trackers, logs, charts, and anything you can come up with to track your progress.

OUTLINE THE MONTH
✓ COMMITMENTS/DUE DATES
✓ DEFINE GOALS
✓ ACTION PLAN FOR EACH GOAL
✓ CREATE NECESSARY TRACKERS

The idea behind this monthly session is to strategize and be prepared for the upcoming month. You can make this as long or as short as you want. If what I mentioned is too much planning you for you, that's okay. Start with the basics: your commitments and maybe only one goal with its corresponding tracker. That's more than enough.

In my life, this planning routine is a creative outlet. This is where I take out all of my journaling supplies. I come up with and research a theme or color scheme, and I get creative with my spreads and trackers. I love the feeling of incorporating art into my planning system, and this is where I go crazy.

Regardless of whether or not that's your thing, it's pretty practical to already have all of your trackers and intentions for the month set up, so all that's left is to act! What will you outline each month?

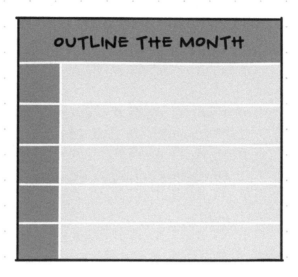

PLAN THE WEEK

A solid action plan has a date and time. The weekly routine is where you solidify your plans. The general outline of your month will come in handy when you're planning out your weeks. The idea is to transfer those plans into your daily life. So, how do we do that?

Let's say it's Sunday, which in my little world equals official weekly planning day. In a maximum fifteen-minute session, I reflect on the previous week—because this is crucial to staying on top of your life—and plan for the upcoming one. This Weekly Check In allows me to reset before the week starts. This is where you might want to look back at the goals list for the month and transfer the outcomes you want to achieve that week onto your Weekly Board. For example: May 2020 goals: Finish writing JPM. Week 20 Outcome: Write Chapter 16. Refer to your Monthly Log and organize what you'll do (and when) for the next seven days.

This Check In session should simple. Look back over the month's outline and plan the upcoming week. Period. The more you practice pausing to plan, the easier it'll become. The way to do that is by making a routine out of it, something you do every Sunday night, or Monday morning, or whatever suits your schedule. Start small, and maybe after you've tackled the Weekly Check In, start building a Sunday Reset Routine that will give you an ever greater clean slate feeling.

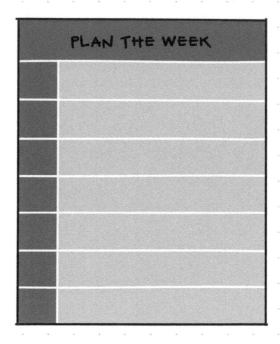

EXECUTE TODAY

It helps if you start the day on the right foot. A morning routine makes that a whole lot easier. But, if you're not ready for that, it's okay. You can start by just checking in with your journal in the morning. Write today's date, and there, you've got yourself a Daily Log. Take a minute to look back at your Weekly Board so you know what it is you're supposed to be doing today. Maybe go as far as writing in the "One Big Thing" you want to accomplish today. That's enough to get you started and shouldn't take more than three minutes.

If you're a pro at using your Daily Log, go crazy! Organize your day, capture all your thoughts, and keep your journal with you at all times. Use it. Get in the habit of using it as your second brain.

Thought, dot journal. Thought, dot journal. Just write. And remember: honor your commitments, focus on what matters, and stay true to who you are. Once you've gotten used to using your Daily Log, you might want to incorporate a little sorting session to your Sunday Reset where you can migrate what's out of place into its proper list.

Journal when you need to, and appreciate the fact that a ten-minute writing session could completely flip your mood around and bring you calm.

Once the day is coming to an end, as part of your evening routine—if you have one—check back in with your journal. This is when you log all you habits and fill in any trackers. Reflect a little bit upon your day. Get in the habit of opening your journal before you go to sleep, so you wake up ready for the next day. It doesn't have to take long and it doesn't have to be fancy. It just has to be intentional. Do whatever you need in the moment.

EXECUTE TODAY	
MORNING	
✓	GRATITUDE/GOALS/INTENTION
✓	ONE BIG THING
✓	TODAY'S TO-DO LIST
EVENING	
✓	TODAY'S WINS
✓	LOG HABITS
✓	OUTLINE TOMORROW

If incorporating all of this into your life seems like too much at the moment, start with these a.m. and p.m. Reflections. Five minutes in the morning and five minutes at night of intentional planning is all you need to get started on this next chapter of your life.

```
┌─────────────────────────────────────┐
│          EXECUTE TODAY              │
├─────────────────────────────────────┤
│ MORNING                             │
├────┬────────────────────────────────┤
│    │                                │
├────┼────────────────────────────────┤
│    │                                │
├────┼────────────────────────────────┤
│    │                                │
├────┴────────────────────────────────┤
│ EVENING                             │
├────┬────────────────────────────────┤
│    │                                │
├────┼────────────────────────────────┤
│    │                                │
├────┼────────────────────────────────┤
│    │                                │
└────┴────────────────────────────────┘
```

CONCLUSION

It's Your Turn

This is it. You know exactly what you have to do. Before you go, I want to leave you with one last piece of advice.

"Planning is everything, the plan is nothing."

—Dwight Eisenhower

Know that your plan will most likely not go as you predicted. Life happens. This, however, does not diminish the value of making a plan. Planning is just a means of being prepared. What matters the most is being mentally, physically, and emotionally primed to handle any curve balls life throws at you. Through planning, through routines, and through creating yourself, you can make sure that you're always ready.

The fun part of life is discovering and creating who you are. You have what you need. So, go. Chase your dreams, achieve your goals, create memories, and write it all down in a little 5" by 8" dotted journal. Fill the pages, pour out your emotions, and outline your life. Because you can do it. You can be the best version of yourself. You can have the life you want. That's the magic of planning.

Glossary

Airing Your Ambitions: Putting your goals out into the world where you can be reminded of them and review your progress on a regular basis

Batching: Combining similar tasks (in content, materials needed, or workflow) into a batch and working on them for a dedicated period of time.

Battle Blueprint: Designating an action for each goal.

Calendar Blocking: Assigning a date and time to specific tasks and blocking that time in your calendar.

Collection: A page with a title made specifically for logging content related to that title.

Current Goals: Something you want more of or less of in your life.

Daily Log: A collection with the day's date as a title that serves a "catchall for Rapid Logging your thoughts throughout the day."

Future Log: A collection for your future commitments.

Goal Gathering: Refining your goals and creating inspiring statements from them.

Grid Map: A breakdown of the number of rows and columns *your* journal contains, along with some of the most common ways of dividing the page.

Habit Tracker: A chart with the list of habits on one axis and the days of the week/month/year on the other.

Ladder Goals: Long term projects with multiple steps or subtasks.

Migration: The process of filtering and sorting your journal.

Milestone Map: A timeline with due dates and potential milestones for a long term goals or project.

Mise-en-place: A culinary process in which ingredients are prepared and organized before cooking. In terms of an evening routine, this means setting everything up so it's ready to go the next day.

Monthly Log: A collection with the dates of the current month.

Proactive Mode: Acting before a situation becomes urgent.

Productive Momentum: The momentum gained when you start accomplishing tasks that will motivate you to keep accomplishing tasks.

Rapid Logging: "Using short-form notation paired with symbols to quickly capture, categorize, and prioritize your thoughts into Notes, Events, and Tasks." —Ryder Carroll

Reactive Mode: Reacting to the past/present rather than anticipating the future.

Reflection: The practice of logging and revising your journal without other distractions.

Someday Goal: Something you can do in one day that doesn't need much planning or effort.

Sometime Soon List: A list of tasks or mini-projects that you want to get to sometime soon.

Spread: A page you've created in your journal.

Sunday Reset: A weekly routine to create a fresh start for the upcoming week, composed of a Recap, Reset, Restart, and Recharge list.

Symbolic Start: An activity performed during your evening routine that helps you transition from a busy workday into a relaxed mood. Can be used for the morning routine as well for transitioning from a sleepy mood into a productive mood.

The Habit Loop: Cue, Craving, Routine, Reward.

The Principles of Productivity: Honor your commitments. Embrace your Chronotype (stay true to who you are). Let go of the Busy Identity (focus on what matters).

Threading: Connecting collections by adding a dot plus the page number of where the collection continues next to that page's number.

Time Travel: Reviewing progress and visualizing the future to figure out what your possible goals are.

Twenty Second Rule: Reduce the amount of time it takes to get into a positive habit to, ideally, less than twenty seconds.

Two Minute Rule: Scale down any habit so that it takes two minute or less to perform.

Weekly Board: A spread to plan ahead for the next seven days, composed of the events, tasks, goals, and anything else you want to track for the upcoming week.

Weekly Check In: The process of reflecting on the previous week and planning ahead for the next one by doing the Weekly Recap, sorting through your journal, and creating the Weekly Board.

Weekly Log: A two-page spread that contains all seven Daily Logs, set up at the beginning of the week in planner format.

Weekly Recap: A set of questions that review the previous week.

Acknowledgments

What a journey this has been, and I have so many people to thank for it.

First, to my boyfriend, Javier Rios: Thank you for being the voice outside my head. The number of hours you've listened to me blabber on and on about this book is something I could never make up for. Thank you for reading so many pages about a topic you couldn't care less about. Thank you for being my rock and my best friend. Thank for your never-ending support. I couldn't have done this without you.

To my brother, Ricar: Thank you for showing me what it means to share and live your passion every day of your life. You inspired to me do the same for no reason other than because it makes me happy. I wouldn't be here without you.

To my personal cheerleaders, Diana Zamora and Gabriela Arce: Thank you for believing in me. Thank you for listening to me for hours on end. Thank you for always helping me when I needed guidance or support. It's because of you that I know that my crazy ideas are worth sharing. Thank you for being a part of this journey. To true friendship.

To my Mom: Thank you for everything. Thank you for raising me, thank you for supporting me, thank you for loving me. I am who I am because of you. I am where I am because of you. Thank you for pushing me when I needed it and for always believing that I can live up to my potential.

To my stepfather, Mano: Thank you for being a true parent. You've shaped who I am in more ways than you can imagine. Thank you for your patience, encouragement, and for always believing in me.

To my Dad: I wish I could share this moment with you. There are so many things that you've taught me, and so many memories I'll never forget. Thank you for still being a guide in my life. Thank you for always telling me that I could do anything, yet bringing me back to earth in the same conversation. Thank you for showing me how to be happy.

To my sisters, Gaby & Vivi: Thank you for always supporting me in my crazy ideas. Thank you for listening to what I have to say and making working on these little projects of mine fun. I can't wait to share more with you.

To my amazing editor, Natasha, without whom this wouldn't be possible: Thank you so much for your guidance during this process. Thank you for giving me this opportunity and believing in me. Thank you for your huge patience and encouraging words. Thank you for listening to my ideas and caring so much about this project. This book would not be the same without you.

To the entire team at Mango Publishing: Thank you for giving me a voice and letting me share a part of my story. Thank you for your support and guidance. Working with you has been a pleasure.

Finally, to my entire family: I can't write all of your names because I would fill a few pages, but you know who you are (best friends included). Thank you for teaching so much about life and for wanting to hear what I have to say. Thank you for your endless love and support. Thank you for the experiences and memories and for being a part of who I am. I've learned so much from you, and I hope we all continue to grow together.

References

Achor, Shawn. 2010. *The Happiness Advantage.* New York: Broadway Books.

Allen, David. 2003. *Getting Things Done: The Art of Stress-free Productivity.* New York: Penguin.

Bailey, Chris. 2017. *The Productivity Project.* New York: Crown.

Benjamin Harkin, Thomas L Webb, Betty P I Chang, Andrew Prestwich Mark Conner, Ian Kellar, Yael Benn, Paschal Sheeran. 2015. *Does Monitoring Goal Progress Promote Goal Attainment? A Meta-Analysis of the Experimental Evidence.* October 19. Accessed February 25, 2020. https://pubmed.ncbi.nlm.nih.gov/26479070/.

Cameron, Julia. 1992. *The Artist's Way.* Los Angeles: Jeremy P. Tarcher/Perigee.

Carroll, Ryder. 2018. *The Bullet Journal Method: Track the Past, Order the Present, Design the Future.* New York: New York: Portfolio/Penguin.

Clear, James. 2018. *Atomic Habits.* New York: Avery, an imprint of Penguin Random House.

Covey, Stephen R. 2004. *The 7 Habits Of Highly Effective People: Restoring The Character Ethic.* New York: Free Press.

Daharsh, Carlin. 2014. *Too Busy for Productivity.* Performed by Carlin Daharsh. Lied Center for Performing Arts, Nebraska. September.

Deloitte Global Mobile Consumer Survey. 2017. *2017 Global Mobile Consumer Survey: US edition. The dawn of the next era in mobile.*

Drew, Nathaniel. "How I Bullet Journal for more Focus and Productivity." *YouTube* video, 7:15. December 12, 2018.

Duhugg, Charles. 2012. *The Power of Habit.* New York: Random House.

Harvey, Lexie. 2016. *The Busy Identity.* Performed by Lexie Harvey. TEDxFurmanU, Nashville. April.

James, William. 1890. *Principles of Psychology.* New York: H. Holt and Company.

Katherine A. Kaplan, David C. Talavera, Allison G. Harvey. 2018. *Rise and Shine: A Treatment Experiment Testing a Morning Routine to Decrease Subjective Sleep Inertia in Insomnia and Bipolar Disorder.* October 27. Accessed January 10, 2020. https://pubmed.ncbi.nlm.nih.gov/30399503/.

M. E. Jewett, J. K. Wyatt, A. Ritz-De Cecco, S. B. Khalsa, D. J. Dijk, C. A. Czeisler. 1999. *Time Course of Sleep Inertia Dissipation in Human Performance and Alertness.* March. Accessed April 7, 2020. https://pubmed.ncbi.nlm.nih.gov/10188130/.

Mumford, George. 2015. *The Mindful Athlete: Secrets to Pure Performance.* Berkeley: Parallax Press.

Newport, Cal. 2016. *Deep Work: Rules for Focused Success in a Distracted World.* New York: Grand Central Publishing.

Obama, Michelle. 2018. *Becoming.* New York: New York: Crown.

Pink, Daniel H. 2017. *The Scientific Secrets of Perfect Timing.* New York: New York: Riverhead Books.

Rubin, Gretchen. New York. *Outer Order, Inner Calm.* Harmony.

Semeco, Arlene. 2017. *The Top 10 Benefits of Regular Exercise.* February 10. Accessed March 25, 2020. https://www.healthline.com/nutrition/10-benefits-of-exercise.

Sharot, Tali. 2014. *How to Motivate Yourself to Change your Behavior.* Performed by Tali Sharot. TEDxCambridge, Boston. October.

Silwa, Jim. 2015. *Frequently Monitoring Progress Toward Goals Increases Chance of Success.* October 28. Accessed February 18, 2020. https://www.apa.org/news/press/releases/2015/10/progress-goals.

Vaden, Rory. 2015. *How To Multiply Your Time.* Performed by Rory Vaden. TEDxDouglasville, Douglasville. June.

About the Author

Andrea González Vega is a medical student obsessed with the world of self-development. She is the creator of Plan for Productivity, a platform and brand dedicated to helping people chase their dreams and live a fulfilled, intentional life by teaching about mindset, planning, and productivity. This is her first book.

Connect with Andrea for more journal planning magic! You can reach out and share your own planning progress by finding her on:

YouTube: Plan for Productivity

Instagram: @PlanforProductivity

Pinterest: Plan for Productivity

Mango Publishing, established in 2014, publishes an eclectic list of books by diverse authors—both new and established voices—on topics ranging from business, personal growth, women's empowerment, LGBTQ studies, health, and spirituality to history, popular culture, time management, decluttering, lifestyle, mental wellness, aging, and sustainable living. We were recently named 2019 *and* 2020's #1 fastest growing independent publisher by *Publishers Weekly*. Our success is driven by our main goal, which is to publish high quality books that will entertain readers as well as make a positive difference in their lives.

Our readers are our most important resource; we value your input, suggestions, and ideas. We'd love to hear from you—after all, we are publishing books for you!

Please stay in touch with us and follow us at:

Facebook: Mango Publishing
Twitter: @MangoPublishing
Instagram: @MangoPublishing
LinkedIn: Mango Publishing
Pinterest: Mango Publishing
Newsletter: mangopublishinggroup.com/newsletter

Join us on Mango's journey to reinvent publishing, one book at a time.

CPSIA information can be obtained
at www.ICGtesting.com
Printed in the USA
JSHW011440220920
8136JS00003B/3

9 781642 503500